P9-CME-545

C INSTRUMENTS

WITHDRAWN

THE REAL WORSHIP BOOK

ISBN 978-1-4234-3469-6

HAL•LEONARD® CORPORATION

7777 W. BLUEMOUND RD. P.O. BOX 13819 MILWAUKEE, WI 53213

Visit Hal Leonard Online at
www.halleonard.com

PREFACE

The Real Worship Book is the answer for today's worship leaders and bands. It is an alternative to the illegible, inaccurate, poorly edited (and sometimes illegal) lead sheets and chord charts which abound today. The Real Worship Book is accurate, neat, and is designed for practical use. Here are some of the features:

1. FORMAT
   a. The book is professionally copied and meticulously checked for accuracy.
   b. Main sections within each song are clearly marked by double bars.
   c. There are no page turns.
   d. General tempo indications are provided to assist with set selection.
   e. Songs are indexed alphabetically, by key, and by tempo.
   f. Each song includes melody, chords and lyrics.

2. SELECTION OF TUNES AND EDITING
   a. 200 songs are included, representing major songwriters such as Chris Tomlin, Paul Baloche, Matt Redman, and more.
   b. Many of CCLI's top-ranked songs are here, plus a large selection of both new and classic favorites.
   c. A variety of sources were consulted to create standard, user-friendly representations of the songs. Some repeats, interludes, bridges and tags were shortened or omitted to keep the song forms concise.
   d. Songs have been placed in both singable and guitar-friendly keys whenever possible. (Guitar capo chords are provided when needed.)

3. SOURCE REFERENCE
   a. The writer(s) and publisher(s) of each song is cited.
   b. All songs have been fully licensed.

4. RESTRICTIONS
Possession of a CCLI license does not give you permission to copy any material from this book. For information about what is allowed under a CCLI license, please visit www.ccli.com or call 1-800-234-2446.

A

ABOVE ALL...................................... 8

AGAIN I SAY REJOICE........................ 10

AGNUS DEI...................................... 9

ALIVE FOREVER AMEN........................ 12

ALL BECAUSE OF JESUS 14

ALL BOW DOWN................................ 16

ALL THE EARTH WILL SING
    YOUR PRAISES 18

ALL WE NEED.................................. 20

AMAZED 19

AMAZING GRACE
    (MY CHAINS ARE GONE) 22

ANCIENT OF DAYS 24

ANCIENT WORDS.............................. 26

ARISE 28

AT THE CROSS 30

AT THE FOOT OF THE CROSS................ 29

AWESOME GOD................................ 32

AWESOME IS THE LORD MOST HIGH 34

B

BE LIFTED HIGH 33

BE UNTO YOUR NAME........................ 36

BEAUTIFUL ONE.............................. 38

BEAUTIFUL SAVIOR (ALL MY DAYS) 40

BEAUTY OF THE LORD 42

BECAUSE OF YOUR LOVE.................... 44

BEFORE THE THRONE OF GOD ABOVE..... 46

BETTER IS ONE DAY 48

BETTER THAN LIFE 50

BLESS THE LORD 52

BLESSED.. 54

BLESSED BE YOUR NAME 56

BREATHE 43

C

CAME TO MY RESCUE.......................... 58

CELEBRATE THE LORD OF LOVE 60

CENTER 62

COME, NOW IS THE TIME TO WORSHIP.... 64

COME THOU FOUNT, COME THOU KING.... 66

CONSUMING FIRE.............................. 68

COUNTING ON GOD............................ 70

D

DANCING GENERATION 72

DAYS OF ELIJAH.............................. 74

DRAW ME CLOSE 76

E

ENOUGH.. 78

EVERLASTING GOD 80

EVERYTHING 61

EVERYTHING GLORIOUS 82

F

FACEDOWN...................................... 84

FAMOUS ONE 86

FILLED WITH YOUR GLORY 88

FOR ALL YOU'VE DONE 90

FOR WHO YOU ARE 92

FOREVER.. 94

F (cont.)

FRIEND OF GOD 96

FROM THE INSIDE OUT 98

FROM THE RISING.......................... 100

G

GIVE THANKS 102

GIVE US CLEAN HANDS 104

GLORY IN THE HIGHEST 106

GLORY TO GOD FOREVER 108

GOD IS GREAT.......................... 110

GOD OF THIS CITY 112

GOD OF WONDERS.......................... 114

GRACE FLOWS DOWN 116

GREAT IS THE LORD 118

H

HAPPY DAY 120

HE IS EXALTED 103

HEAR OUR PRAISES.......................... 122

HEAR US FROM HEAVEN.......................... 124

THE HEART OF WORSHIP.......................... 126

HERE I AM TO WORSHIP.......................... 128

HERE IN YOUR PRESENCE.......................... 130

HERE IS OUR KING 132

HIDING PLACE 125

HOLY IS THE LORD 134

HOLY IS YOUR NAME.......................... 136

HOLY SPIRIT RAIN DOWN.......................... 138

HOSANNA 140

HOSANNA (PRAISE IS RISING) 142

HOW CAN I KEEP FROM SINGING.......................... 144

HOW DEEP THE FATHER'S
LOVE FOR US.......................... 146

HOW GREAT IS OUR GOD.......................... 148

HOW HE LOVES 150

I

I AM FREE.......................... 152

I COULD SING OF YOUR
LOVE FOREVER 154

I GIVE YOU MY HEART 156

I KNOW WHO I AM.......................... 158

I WILL BOAST 147

I WILL CALL UPON THE LORD.......................... 160

I WILL EXALT YOUR NAME.......................... 161

I WILL RISE 162

IN CHRIST ALONE 164

INDESCRIBABLE.......................... 166

IT IS YOU.......................... 168

J

JESUS, ALL FOR JESUS 170

JESUS, DRAW ME CLOSE.......................... 172

JESUS LORD OF HEAVEN.......................... 174

JESUS, LOVER OF MY SOUL.......................... 173

JESUS MESSIAH.......................... 176

THE JOY OF THE LORD.......................... 178

K

KING OF MAJESTY.......................... 180

L

LEAD ME TO THE CROSS.......................... 182

LET EVERYTHING THAT HAS BREATH .. 184

LET GOD ARISE.......................... 186

LET IT RISE 188

LET MY WORDS BE FEW
(I'LL STAND IN AWE OF YOU).......................... 189

LET THE CHURCH RISE.......................... 190

LET THE PRAISES RING 192

LORD, I LIFT YOUR NAME ON HIGH 194

LORD, REIGN IN ME.......................... 196

LORD, YOU HAVE MY HEART 195

LOVE THE LORD.......................... 198

M

MADE ME GLAD 200

MADE TO WORSHIP 202

MAJESTIC 204

MAJESTY (HERE I AM) 206

MARVELOUS LIGHT 208

MIGHTY IS THE POWER OF
      THE CROSS 210

MIGHTY TO SAVE 212

THE MORE I SEEK YOU 205

MORE PRECIOUS THAN SILVER 214

MY HOPE IS YOU 216

MY REDEEMER LIVES 218

MY SAVIOR LIVES 220

MY SAVIOR MY GOD 222

N

NEW DOXOLOGY 215

A NEW HALLELUJAH 224

NO ONE LIKE YOU 226

NO SWEETER NAME 228

NONE BUT JESUS 230

NOT TO US 232

NOTHING BUT THE BLOOD 234

O

O CHURCH ARISE 236

O PRAISE HIM
      (ALL THIS FOR A KING) 238

OFFERING 240

OH HOW HE LOVES YOU AND ME 237

ON THE THIRD DAY 242

ONCE AGAIN 244

ONE WAY 246

OPEN THE EYES OF MY HEART 248

OUR GOD SAVES 250

OUR GREAT GOD 252

P

THE POWER OF THE CROSS
      (OH TO SEE THE DAWN) 254

PROMISES 256

R

REDEEMER, SAVIOR, FRIEND 255

RESCUE 258

REVELATION SONG 260

REVIVAL 262

RISE UP AND PRAISE HIM 264

S

SALT AND LIGHT 266

SALVATION IS HERE 268

SAVIOUR KING 270

SAY SO 272

SHINE 274

SHINE, JESUS, SHINE 269

SHOUT TO THE LORD 276

SHOUT TO THE NORTH 278

SING FOR JOY 280

SING, SING, SING 282

SING TO THE KING 284

SON OF GOD 286

SPEAK O LORD 281

THE STAND 288

STEP BY STEP 290

STILL 291

STRONG TOWER 292

SWEETER 294

T

TAKE ME IN 296

TAKE MY LIFE 298

THANK YOU, LORD 300

THERE IS A HIGHER THRONE 302

T (cont.)

THERE IS A REDEEMER 297

THERE IS JOY IN THE LORD 304

TIL I SEE YOU 306

TO THE ONLY GOD 308

TODAY IS THE DAY 310

U

UNCHANGING 312

UNDIGNIFIED 314

UNFAILING LOVE 316

W

WE FALL DOWN 309

WE GIVE YOU GLORY 318

WE WANT TO SEE JESUS
    LIFTED HIGH 320

WE WILL WORSHIP HIM 322

WHAT CAN I DO? 323

WHEN IT'S ALL BEEN SAID
    AND DONE 324

WHOLLY YOURS 326

THE WONDERFUL CROSS 328

WONDERFUL MAKER 330

WONDERFUL, MERCIFUL SAVIOR 332

WORTHY IS THE LAMB 334

Y

YESTERDAY, TODAY AND FOREVER 336

YOU ALONE 338

YOU ARE GOD ALONE (NOT A GOD) 340

YOU ARE GOOD 342

YOU ARE MY ALL IN ALL 344

YOU ARE MY KING (AMAZING LOVE) ... 346

YOU GAVE YOUR LIFE AWAY 348

YOU NEVER LET GO 350

YOU, YOU ARE GOD 352

YOU'RE WORTHY OF MY PRAISE 354

YOUR GRACE IS ENOUGH 356

YOUR LOVE IS DEEP 358

YOUR NAME 345

KEY INDEX 360

TEMPO INDEX 364

MORE WORSHIP RESOURCES 367

AGAIN I SAY REJOICE

Israel Houghton / Aaron Lindsey

12

Alive Forever Amen

– Travis Cottrell/Sue C. Smith/David Moffitt

(MID/UP)

Let the chil-dren sing a song of lib-er-a-tion;
Let my heart sing out, for Christ, the One and on-ly,

the God of our sal-va-tion set us free.
so pow-er-ful and ho-ly, res-cued me.

Death, where is thy sting? The curse of sin is bro-ken.
Death won't hurt me now be-cause He has re-deemed me.

The emp-ty tomb stands o-pen; come and see. He's a-live,
No grave will ev-er keep me from my King. I'm a-live,

a-live, a-live, hal-le-lu-jah. A-live,

praise and glo-ry to the Lamb. A-live,

All Bow Down

— Chris Tomlin / Ed Cash

(MID/UP)

16

You're ar-riv - ing with the sound of thun - der and rain.
Praise a - waits You at the dawn when the world comes a - live.
You are com - ing a - gain like a thief in the night.

You're ar-riv - ing in the calm of the wind and the waves.
Praise a - waits You in the dark - ness and shines in the light.
You are com - ing a - gain with a shout from the sky.

You're ar-riv - ing in the glow of a burn - ing flame,
Praise a - waits You with a song
You are com - ing a - gain

a burn - ing flame. of love and de - si -

- re, love and de - si - re.

To Chorus

Here comes the King; to take a - way Your bride, to take a - way Your bride.

CHORUS

All The Earth Will Sing Your Praises

-Paul Baloche

AMAZED

— JARED ANDERSON

20

All We Need

— Charlie Hall

A/C#

my hands can hold, my heart, mind and strength and soul.

Bm7

D.S. AL ⊕
(TAKE REPEAT)

G

Be my all, all - con - sum - ing fire. 'Cause we

G

D

All we need, all we need,

A

Bm7

all we need is You.

G

2. G

All we need,

22

Amazing Grace
(My Chains Are Gone)

~John Newton / Chris Tomlin / Louie Giglio

ANCIENT OF DAYS

— Gary Sadler / Jamie Harvill

roam,   an - cient   words will guide   us   home.}   An - cient
heart.   Oh, let   the   an - cient words   im -   part.}

words,   ev - er   true,   chang-ing   me   and chang-ing   you.   We have

come   with   o - pen hearts.   Oh,   let   the   an - cient words   im -

part.   Ho - ly___   part.   An - cient

part._____

Arise

At the Foot of the Cross

– Kathryn Scott

(Slow/Mid)

At the foot of the cross, ___ where grace ___ and suf - f'ring meet, ___
(At the foot of the cross,) ___ where I ___ am made com - plete, ___

You have shown me Your love ___ through the judg -
You have giv - en me life ___ through the death ___

- ment You ___ re - ceived. ___ }
You bore ___ for me. ___ } And You've won ___ my heart,

and You've won ___ my heart. Now I can

trade these ash - es in - to beau - ty, and wear for - give - ness like a

crown. Com - ing to kiss the feet of Mer - cy, I lay

ev - 'ry bur - den down ___ at the foot of the cross. ___

1. G

2. G

At the foot of the cross, _ ___

At the Cross

— Reuben Morgan / Darlene Zschech

(Slow/Mid)

O Lord,— You've searched— me,— You know— my ways..

E - ven when— I fail— You,—

I know— You love me.— Your ho — ly pres -
You go— be - fore
And when— the earth

- ence— sur - round - ing me;—
me,— You shield— my way.—
fades,— falls from— my eyes,—

in ev - 'ry sea - son,— I know— You
Your hand— up - holds— me;—
and You stand— be - fore— me,—

love me.— At the cross I bow my knee, where Your blood was shed for

Awesome God

- Rich Mullins

BE LIFTED HIGH

(Slow/Mid.)

—LEELAND MOORING

Additional Lyrics

3. And even now that I'm inside Your hands,
Help me not to grow prideful again.
Don't let me forsake sacrifice.
Jesus, You be lifted high.

4. And if I'm blessed with the riches of kings,
How could I ever think that it was me?
For You brought me from darkness to light.
Jesus, You be lifted high.
(To Chorus)

34

Be Unto Your Name

— Lynn DeShazo / Gary Sadler

(Slow/Mid.)

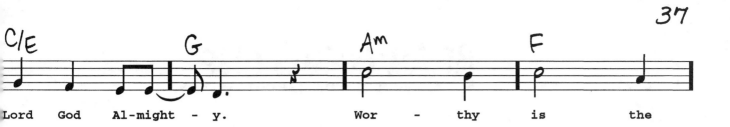

Lord God Al-might - y.   Wor - thy is the

Lamb who was slain.   High - est prais - es,

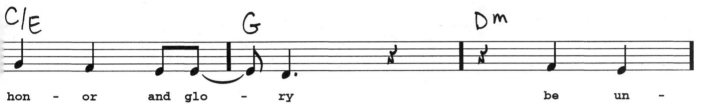

hon - or and glo - ry   be un -

to Your name._____   be un -

to Your name._____

Beautiful One

—Tim Hughes

Won - der - ful, so won - der - ful is Your un - fail - ing
Pow - er - ful, so pow - er - ful, Your glo - ry fills the

___ love. Your cross has spo - ken mer - cy o - ver me.
___ skies, Your might - y works dis - played for all to see.

No eye has seen, no ear has heard, no
The beau - ty of Your maj - es - ty a -

heart could ful - ly___ know how glo - ri - ous, how
wakes my heart to___ sing: How mar - vel - ous, how

beau - ti - ful You___ are.___ }
won - der - ful You___ are.___ } Beau - ti - ful

One I love,___ Beau - ti - ful One I a - dore, Beau - ti - ful

One, my soul must___ sing.___

BEAUTIFUL SAVIOR
(ALL MY DAYS)

- STUART TOWNEND

(SLOW)

All____ my days I will sing this song of
I____ will trust in the cross of my Re-
long____ to be where the praise is nev - er-

glad - ness, give____ my praise to the
deem - er, I____ will sing of the
end - ing, yearn____ to dwell where the

Foun - tain of de - lights. For in my
blood that nev - er fails, of sins my
glo - ry nev - er fades, where count - less

help - less - ness You heard my____ cry, and
giv - en, of con - science____ cleansed, of
wor - ship - ers will share one____ song, and

waves of mer - cy poured__down on my life.____
death de - feat - ed and__ life with - out end.____
cries of "Wor - thy!" will__ hon - or the Lamb.____

Beau - ti - ful Sav - ior,

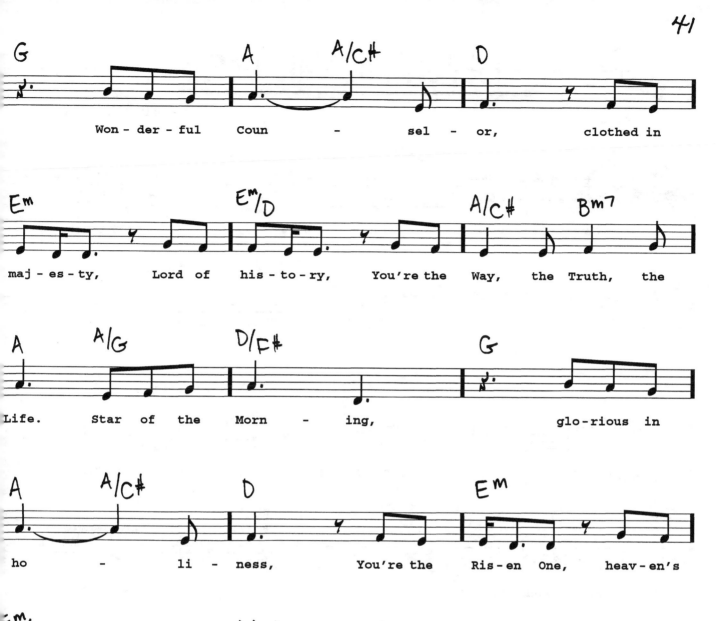

Won - der - ful Coun - sel - or, clothed in

maj - es - ty, Lord of his - to - ry, You're the Way, the Truth, the

Life. Star of the Morn - ing, glo - rious in

ho - li - ness, You're the Ris - en One, heav - en's

Cham - pi - on, and You reign, You reign o - ver_

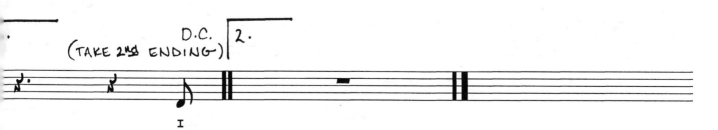

all!

(TAKE 2nd ENDING) D.C. |2.

I

BEAUTY OF THE LORD

(SLOW)

—JARED ANDERSON

BREATHE

— Marie Barnett

(SLOW)

This is__ the air__ I breathe,__ this is__ the air__ I breathe,__ Your ho - ly pres- -ence liv - ing in me.__

This is__ my dai - ly bread,__ this is__ my dai- -ly bread,__ Your ver - y Word__ spo - ken to me.__ And I,__ I'm des - p'rate for__ You.__ And I,__ I'm lost with - out__ You.__

44

Because Of Your Love

- Paul Baloche / Brenton Brown

As we come in-to__ Your pres - ence,__ we re-mem - ber ev - 'ry bless - ing__ that You've poured out__ so free - ly from__ a - bove.__ Lift-ing grat - i - tude__ and prais - es__ for com - pas - sion, so__ a - maz - ing.__ Lord, we've come to give__ You thanks__ for all__ You've__ done.

Be-cause of Your love,__

46

(SLOW/MID) BEFORE THE THRONE OF GOD ABOVE

— Vikki Cook / Charitie Bancroft

Be - fore the throne of God a - bove, I have a
(When Sa - tan) tempts me to de - spair and tells me
(Be - hold Him) there, the ris - en Lamb, my per - fect,

strong and per - fect plea: a great High Priest whose name is
of the guilt with - in, up - ward I look and see Him
spot - less right-eous - ness, the great un - change - a - ble I

Love, who ev - er lives and pleads for me. My name is
there, who made an end of all my sin. Be - cause the
AM, the King of glo - ry and of grace. One with Him -

grav - en on His hands, my name is writ - ten on His
sin - less Sav - ior died, my sin - ful soul is count - ed
self, I can - not die. My soul is pur - chased by His

heart. I know that while in heav'n He stands, no tongue can
free. For God the Just is sat - is - fied to look on
blood. My life is hid with Christ on high, with Christ, my

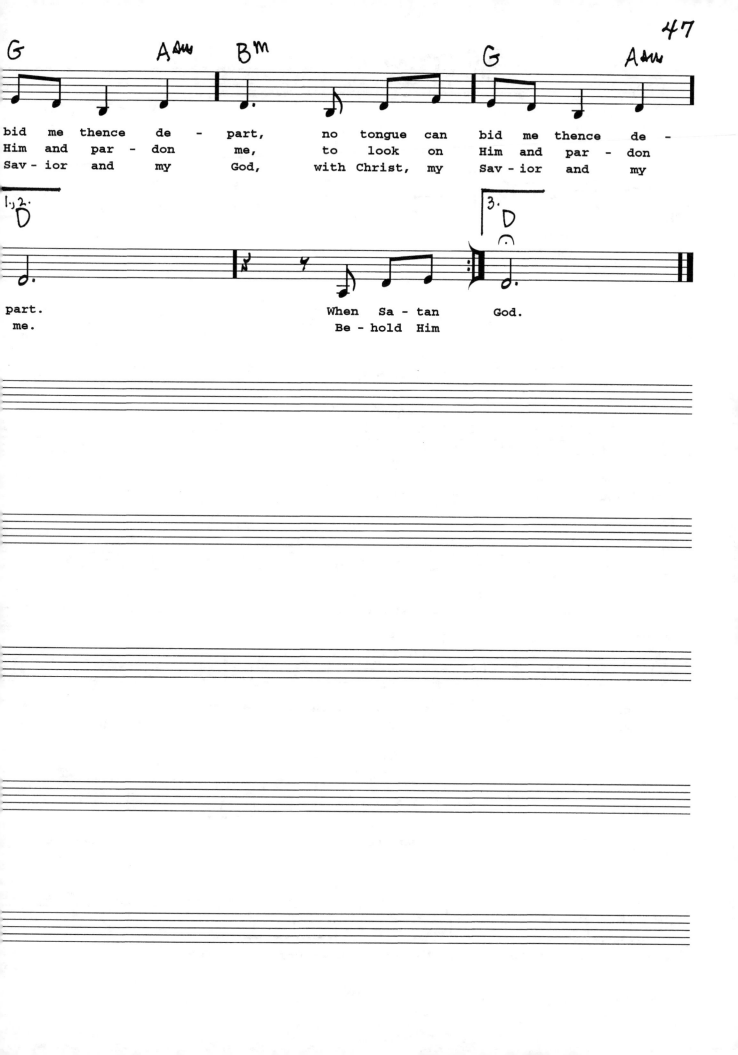

47

G   A⁴ᵐ   B᷾ᵐ   G   A⁴ᵐ

bid me thence de - part,   no tongue can   bid me thence de -
Him and par - don me,   to look on   Him and par - don
Sav - ior and my God,   with Christ, my   Sav - ior and my

1.,2.   3.
D   D

part.   When Sa - tan   God.
me.   Be - hold Him

BETTER IS ONE DAY

— MATT REDMAN

Better Than Life

— Israel Houghton / Cindy Cruse-Ratcliff

lov - ing___ kind - ness is bet-ter than life.
lov - ing___ kind - ness is bet-ter than life.

oh, _____

___ it's bet - ter, oh, _____ bet - ter than life,___

oh, _____ so___ much bet - ter. Je -

- sus, Your lov - ing kind - ness___ is bet - ter than

1.
life.

2.
life. Bet - ter than life.

Bet - ter than life.

52

Bless The Lord

- JEFF DEYO

BLESSED

— Reuben Morgan / Darlene Zschech

56

Blessed Be Your Name

-Matt Redman/Beth Redman

(MID/UP)

Bless - ed be Your name in the land that is plen -
Bless - ed be Your name when the sun's shin - ing down.

- ti - ful, where Your streams of a - bun -
on me, when the world's "all as it

- dance flow, bless - ed be Your name.
should be," bless - ed be Your name.

Bless - ed be Your name when I'm
Bless - ed be Your name on the

found in the des - ert place, tho' I
road marked with suf - fer - ing, tho' there's

walk through the wil - der - ness, bless -
pain in the of - fer - ing, bless -

ed be Your name.
ed be Your name.

Ev - 'ry bless - ing

57

Celebrate The Lord Of Love

— Paul Baloche / Ed Kerr

EVERYTHING

(SLOW)

— ISRAEL HOUGHTON

62

CENTER

— Charlie Hall / Matt Redman

64

70

COUNTING ON GOD

— JARED ANDERSON

Dancing Generation

— Matt Redman

Your mer - cy taught us how to dance,_ to cel - e - brate with all we have,_ and__we'll dance___ to thank___ You for mer - cy. Your glo - ry taught us how to shout,_ to lift Your name in all the earth,_ and__we'll shout___ to the praise___ of Your glo - ry. It's__ the o - ver-flow of a for - giv - en soul. And now we've

73

DAYS OF ELIJAH

—ROBIN MARK

(MID/UP)

DRAW ME CLOSE

—Kelly Carpenter

(SLOW/MID.)

Draw me close_ to You,___ nev-er let_ me go._

I lay it all_ down_ a - gain_ to hear You say_ that I'm_ Your friend._

You are my_ de-sire,_ no one else_ will do._

'Cause noth-ing else_ could take_ Your place,_ to feel the warmth_ of Your_ em - brace._

Help me find_ the way,___ bring me back_ to You._

ENOUGH

Chris Tomlin / Louie Giglio

EVERLASTING GOD

— BRENTON BROWN / KEN RILEY

EVERYTHING GLORIOUS

-David Crowder

So let Your glo - ry shine a - round,_ let Your glo - ry shine a -

ound. King of glo - ry, here be found,_ King of glo - ry.

found,_ King of glo - ry. And I'll

G

ev - 'ry breath   I'm____ prais-ing You.
ev - 'ry eye   is____ watch-ing You.

D

Em

De - sire____ of   na - tions____ and____
Re - vealed____ by   na - ture____ and____

Bm

____ ev - 'ry heart,   You a - lone are God,
____ mir - a - cles,   You are____ beau-ti-ful,

G

A

2nd x , D.C. AL ⊕

You a - lone are God.____
You are beau-ti - ful.____

Filled With Your Glory

-Tim Neufeld / Jon Neufeld

For All You've Done

—Reuben Morgan

for the world__ to live__ a - gain.__ Hal - le - lu -

- jah,_____ for all You've__ done._____

For Who You Are

— Marty Sampson

Forever

—Chris Tomlin

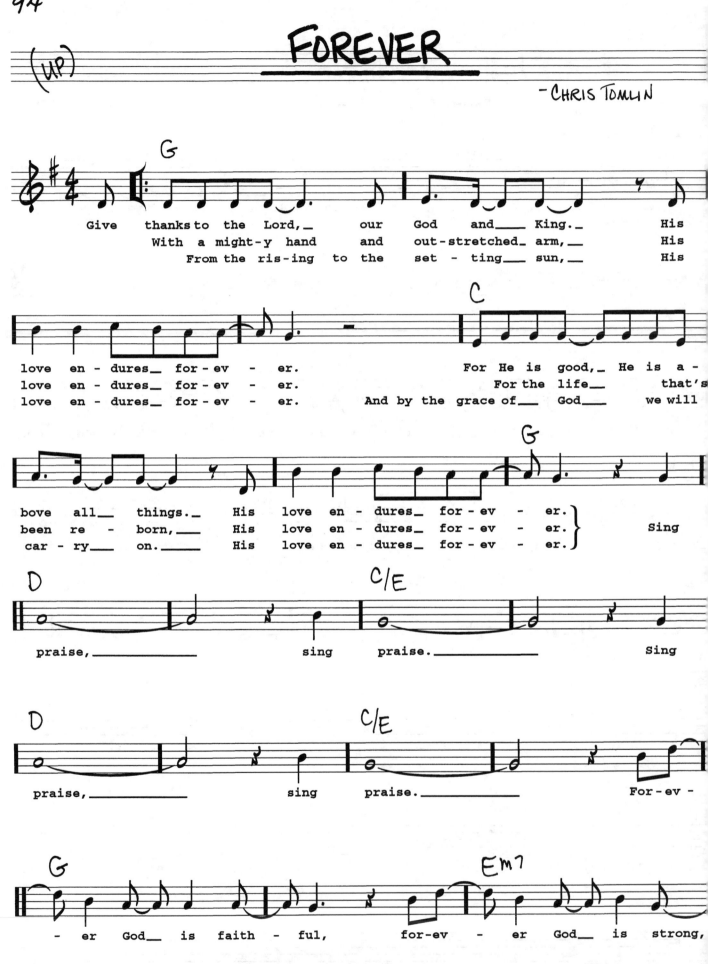

FRIEND OF GOD

— Michael Gungor / Israel Houghton

Who am I that You are mind-ful of me, that You hear me when I call?

Is it true that You are think-ing of me? How You love me, it's a-maz - ing!

I am a friend of God, I am a friend of God, I am a friend of God; He calls me friend.

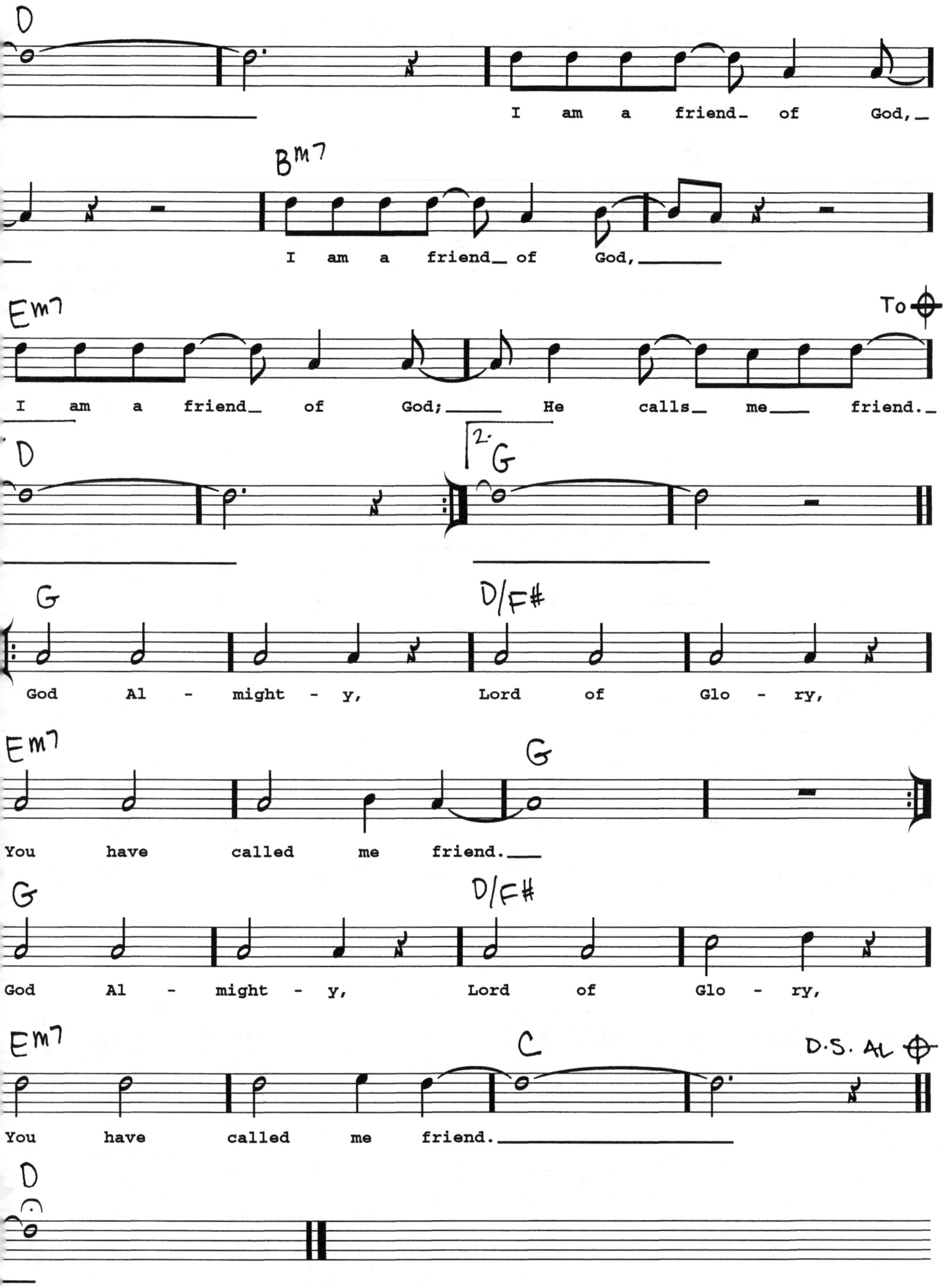

I am a friend of God,

I am a friend of God,

I am a friend of God; He calls me friend.

God Almighty, Lord of Glory,

You have called me friend.

God Almighty, Lord of Glory,

You have called me friend.

From The Rising

— Matt Redman / Paul Baloche

We're gath-ered to wor - ship,_____ be -
(We) gath - er to go_____ out;_____ to

com - ing a choir_____ to sing_____ Your praise,_____
cit - ies and towns,_____ we'll take_____ Your name_____

lift - ing our voic - es,_____
in - to the na - tions,_____

join - ing our hearts_____ in this house_____ to - day._____ }
shin - ing Your light_____ in the dark - est place._____ }

Peo - ple of God,_____ in the pow-er of God,

_____ for the king-dom of God { we sing._____ } From the ris -
{ we live._____ }

HE IS EXALTED

—Twila Paris

(SLOW)

Glory In The Highest

– Chris Tomlin / Jesse Reeves / Daniel Carson / Matt Redman / Ed Cash

high - est,____ glo-ry in the high - est,_

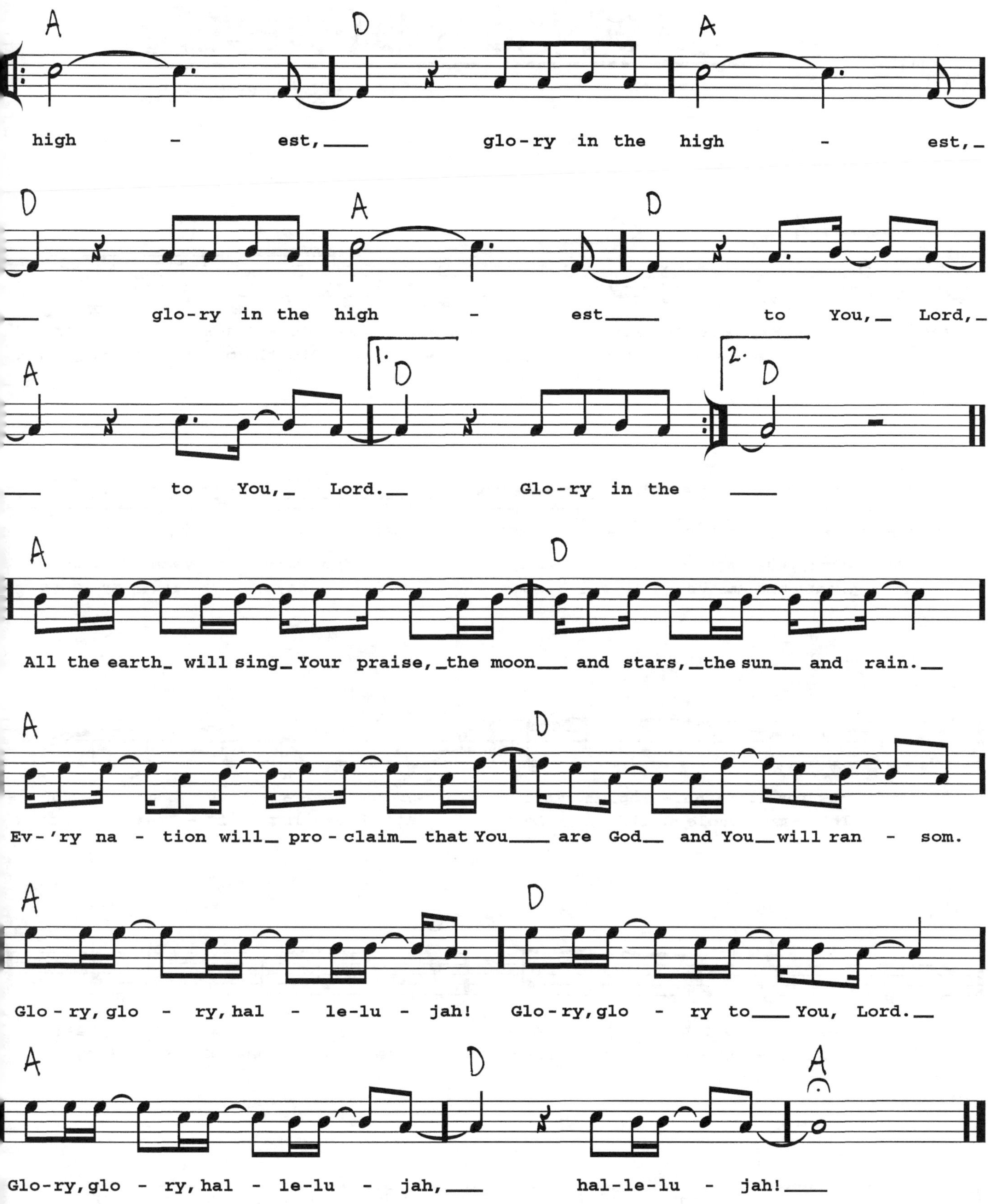

glo-ry in the high - est____ to You,_ Lord,_

to You,_ Lord._ Glo-ry in the ____

All the earth_ will sing_ Your praise,_the moon__ and stars,_the sun__ and rain._

Ev-'ry na - tion will_ pro-claim_ that You__ are God__ and You__will ran - som.

Glo-ry, glo - ry, hal - le-lu - jah! Glo-ry, glo - ry to__ You, Lord._

Glo-ry, glo - ry, hal - le-lu - jah, ____ hal-le-lu - jah!____

GLORY TO GOD FOREVER

— Steve Fee / Vicky Beeching

(MID./UP)

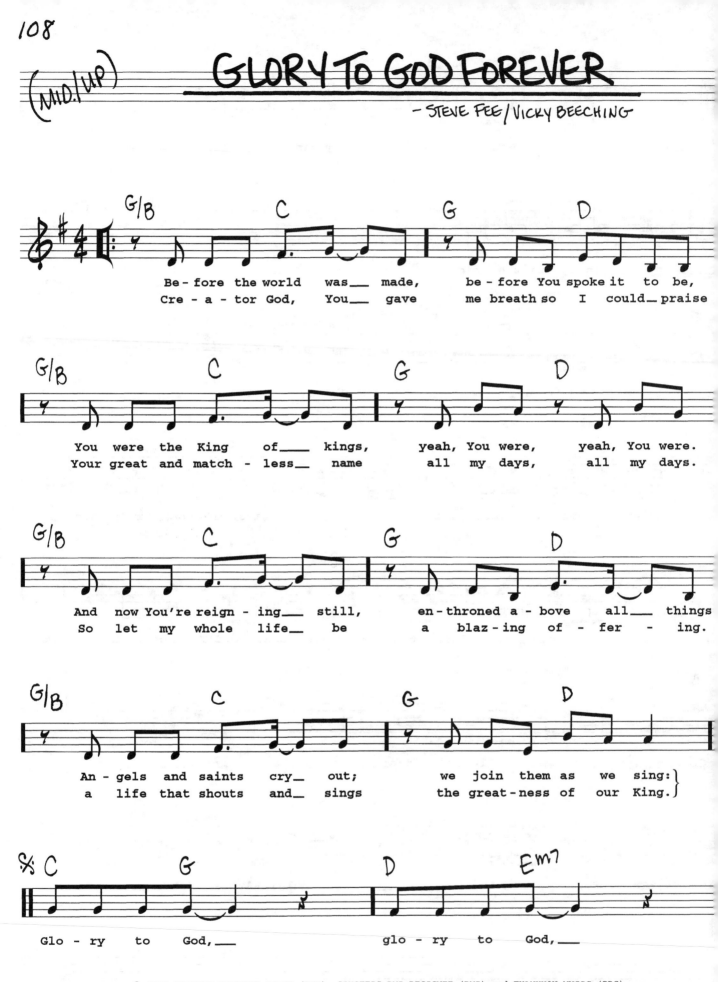

Be-fore the world was__ made, be-fore You spoke it to be,
Cre-a-tor God, You__ gave me breath so I could__ praise

You were the King of__ kings, yeah, You were, yeah, You were.
Your great and match-less__ name all my days, all my days.

And now You're reign-ing__ still, en-throned a-bove all__ things
So let my whole life__ be a blaz-ing of-fer-ing.

An-gels and saints cry__ out; we join them as we sing:
a life that shouts and__ sings the great-ness of our King.

Glo-ry to God, __ glo-ry to God, __

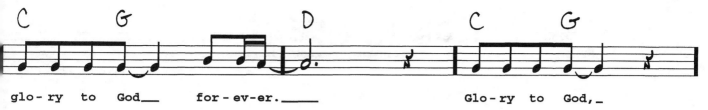

glo - ry to God___ for - ev - er.____ Glo - ry to God, _

glo - ry to God, ___ glo - ry to God___ for - ev - er._

___ Take my life and let it be

all for You and for Your glo - ry. Take my life and let it be Yours._

1. D   2. D   D.S. AL⊕

___   ___   We sing:

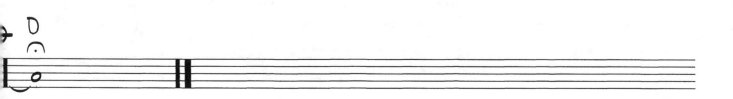

⊕ D

GOD IS GREAT

—MARTY SAMPSON

All cre-a-tion cries to You,____

wor-ship-ing__ in spir-it and__ in truth.__

Glo-ry to____ the faith-ful One,____

Je-sus Christ,__ God's Son.____

All cre-a-tion gives__ You praise.__
All to You,____ O God,__ we bring.__

You a-lone___ are tru-ly great.__
Je-sus, teach__ us how__ to live.__

You a-lone___ are God,__ who reigns____
Let Your fi-re burn__ in us,____ that

There is no one like our God. For

great - er things have yet to come, and great - er things are still to be done in this

cit - y.

Great - er things have yet to come, and great - er things are still to be done in this

cit - y.

You're the God of this

great - er things are still to be done here.

GOD OF WONDERS

-MARC BYRD / STEVE HINDALONG

118

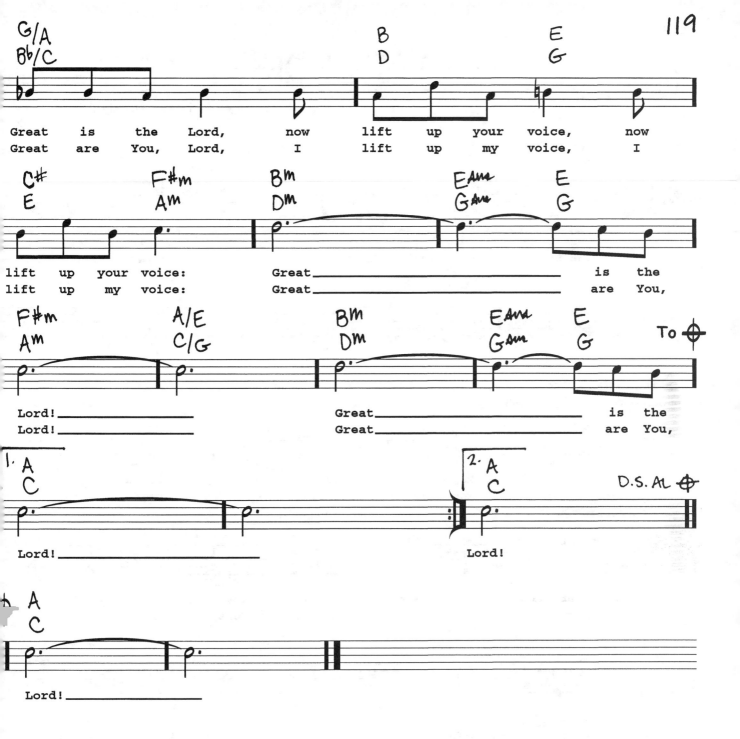

Great is the Lord, now lift up your voice, now
Great are You, Lord, I lift up my voice, I

lift up your voice: Great_____ is the
lift up my voice: Great_____ are You,

Lord!_____ Great_____ is the
Lord!_____ Great_____ are You,

Lord!_____

Lord!

Lord!_____

HAPPY DAY

— Tim Hughes / Ben Cantellon

Great-est day in his-to-ry; death is beat-en, You____
When I stand__ in____ that place, free at last,__ meet-

__ have res-cued me.__ Sing it out: Je - sus is__ a - live.__
-ing face__ to face,__ I am Yours; Je - sus, You__ are mine.

Emp-ty cross, the emp - ty grave,__
End-less joy,___ per - fect peace,__

life e-ter-nal, You____ have won__ the day.__ Shout it out: Je-
earth-ly pain__ fi - nal-ly__ will cease.__ Cel-e-brate, Je-

- sus is__ a - live,__ He's a - live.____
- sus is__ a - live,__ He's a - live.____

And oh,____ hap-py day,__ hap-py day,__ You've washed__

__ my sin a-way. Oh, hap-py day,____ hap-py day,

HEAR OUR PRAISES

—REUBEN MORGAN

126

(SLOW/MID.) THE HEART OF WORSHIP

-MATT REDMAN

When the mu - sic fades,___ all is stripped a - way,___
King of end - less worth,___ no one could ex - press.

and I sim - ply come,___
how much you de - serve.___

long - ing just to bring___ some - thing that's of worth___
Though I'm weak and poor,___ all I have is Yours,

that will bless Your heart.___ }
ev - 'ry sin - gle breath.___ }

I'll bring You more than a song,___ for a song in it - self

is not what You have re - quired.___

You search much deep - er with - in,___ through the way things ap - pear,

129

HERE IN YOUR PRESENCE

—JON EGAN

132

HERE IS OUR KING

(MID/UP)

—David Crowder

From wher-ev-er spring ar-rives to heal the ground,

from wher-ev-er search-ing comes, the look it-self,

a trace of what we're look-ing for. So be qui-et now and wait

The o-cean

is grow-ing, the tide is com-ing in; her

it is. Here is our King, here is our Love, here is our

God who's come to bring us back to Him. He is the One,

He is Je-sus, Je-sus.

134

Holy Is The Lord

— Chris Tomlin / Louie Giglio

(MID.)

We stand and lift up our hands, ___ for the joy ___ of the Lord ___ is our strength. ___ We bow down ___ and wor- ship Him now; ___ how great, ___ how awe - some is He. ___ And to-geth-er we ___ sing: ___ Ho - ly is ___ the Lord God ___ Al-might - y; the earth ___ is filled ___ with His glo- ry. Ho - ly is ___ the Lord God ___ Al-might - y; the earth ___ is filled ___ with His glo -

136

HOLY IS YOUR NAME

— Marc Byrd / Steve Hindalong

138

HOLY SPIRIT RAIN DOWN

(SLOW/MID.)

Russell Fragar

F#7
A7   Bm
      Dm   Am7
      Cm7   G#7b5
      B7b5

no ear has heard,_   no mind can know___   what   God has in store._   So

Gmaj7
Bbmaj7   F#7
      A7   Bm
      Dm

o-pen up heav - en,   o-pen it wide,_   o-ver our church,_   and

1. Am7
   Cm7   G#7b5
      B7b5   2. G/A
      Bb/C   D.S. AL ⊕

o-ver our lives._   o-ver our lives._____   Ho-ly Spir-it,

⊕ D
   F

140

HOSANNA

— Brooke Fraser

(MID.)

142

HOSANNA
(PRAISE IS RISING)

— Paul Baloche / Brenton Brown

(MID./UP)

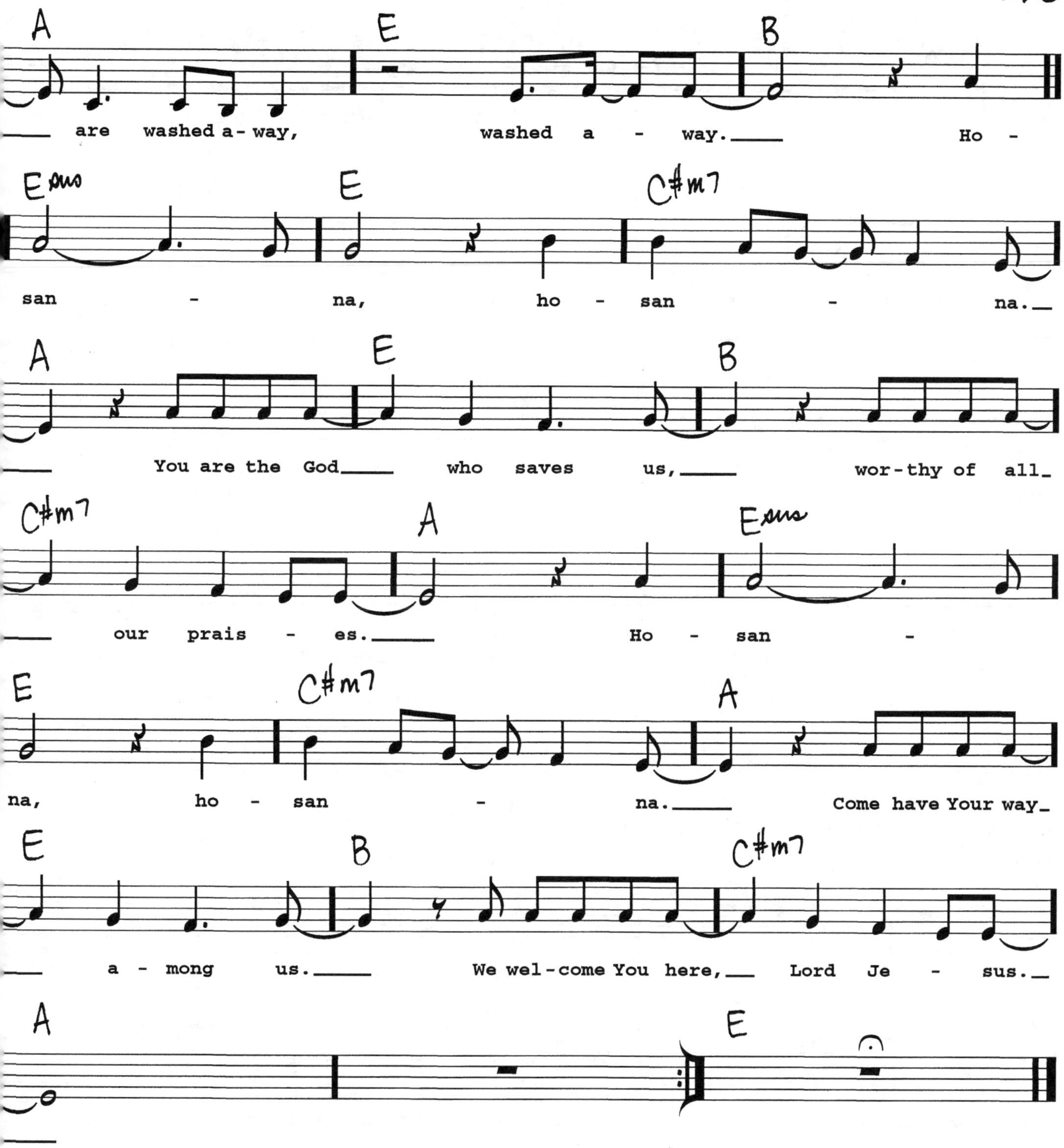

are washed a-way, washed a - way.___ Ho -

san - na, ho - san - na.___

You are the God___ who saves us,___ wor-thy of all___

our prais - es.___ Ho - san -

na, ho - san - na.___ Come have Your way___

a - mong us.___ We wel-come You here,___ Lord Je - sus.___

144

HOW CAN I KEEP FROM SINGING

(Slow/ballad.)

~ Chris Tomlin/Matt Redman/Ed Cash

G
There is an end - less song, ech-oes in my
(I will) lift my eyes in the dark - est

Em ... **C**
soul, I hear the mu - sic ring.
night, for I know my Sav - ior lives.

G ... **D**
And though the storms may come, I am hold - ing
And I will walk with You, know-ing You'll see me

Em **D/F#** **G** **Em** **C**
on; to the rock I cling.
through, and sing the songs You give. }

G ... **D**
How can I keep from sing - ing Your praise? How can I

C **G/B** **C** **D**
ev - er say e - nough? How a - maz - ing is Your love.

G ... **D**
How can I keep from shout - ing Your name? I know I am

C **G/B** **C** **To ⊕ D**
loved by the King, and it makes my heart want to

146

(SLOW)

HOW DEEP THE FATHER'S LOVE FOR US

-STUART TOWNEND

How deep the Fa-ther's love for us, how vast be-yond all meas - ure, that
(Be) - hold the Man up-on a cross, my sin up-on His shoul-ders. A -
(I) will not boast in an-y - thing; no gifts, no pow'r, no wis - dom. But

He should give His on - ly Son to make a wretch His treas - ure. How
shamed, I hear my mock-ing voice call out a-mong the scof - fers. It
I will boast in Je - sus Christ, His death and res - ur - rec - tion. Why

great the pain of sear-ing loss; the Fa-ther turns His face a-way as
was my sin that held Him there un - til it was ac - com - plished; His
should I gain from His re-ward? I can - not give an an - swer. But

wounds which mar the Cho - sen One bring man - y sons to glo -
dy - ing breath has brought me life. I know that it is fin -
this I know with all my heart: His wounds have paid my ran -

ry. Be - som.
ished. I

I WILL BOAST

—PAUL BALOCHE

150

How He Loves

—John Mark McMillan

(SLOW)

He is__ jeal-ous for me.____ Loves like a hur - ri-can

I am a tree,__ bend-ing be-neath__ the weight of His wind and__

mer - cy.__ When all of__ a sud-den,

I am un - a-ware of these af - flic - tions e - clipsed by__

glo - ry,__ and I real-ize__ just how__ beau-ti-ful You are, and how

great Your af-fec - tions are__ for me.__ And oh,

how He__ loves us.__ Oh, oh, how He__

loves__ us,__ how He__ loves us__ all.

152

I AM FREE

—JON EGAN

Through You__ the blind__ will see,__ through You__ the mute__

__ will sing,__ through You__ the dead__ will rise,__

through You__ all hearts__ will praise,__ through You__ the dark -

- ness flees,__ through You__ my heart__ screams, "I am free!

I am free!"__

I am free__ to run.__ (I am

free__ to run.)__ I am free__ to dance.

154

I Could Sing Of Your Love Forever

-Martin Smith

156

I Know Who I Am

Israel Houghton / Chris Tomlin

I know who I am, I know who I am, I know who I am, I am Yours, I am Yours, I I am Yours, and You are mine. Je - sus, You are mine. You are mine Je - sus, You are mine.

I was run - ning and You found me, I was blind - ed
I was bro - ken and You healed me, I was dy - ing
and You gave me sight. You put a song of praise in me.
and You gave me life. Lord, You are my i - den - ti - ty.

Oh, ___

I know, ___ I know. ___ I

I am ___ for - giv - en, ___

I am ___ Your friend, ___ I am ___ ac - cept - ed, ___ I

know who ___ I am. ___ I am ___ se - cure, ___

I'm con - fi - dent ___ that I ___ am loved, ___ I

know who ___ I am. ___ I am ___ a - live, ___

I am ___ set free, ___ I ___ be - long ___ to You ___ and You ___

be - long ___ to me. ___ I

I WILL EXALT YOUR NAME

-JEFFREY B. SCOTT

162

I Will Rise

— Chris Tomlin / Jesse Reeves / Louie Giglio / Matt Maher

(MID.)

In Christ Alone

(SLOW/MID.)

— KEITH GETTY / STUART TOWNEND

| G | D | G | A | D/F# |

In Christ a - lone my hope is found, He is my
(In Christ a) - lone, who took on flesh, full - ness of
(There in the) ground His bod - y lay, Light of the
(No guilt in) life, no fear in death; this is the

| G | D/F# | Em7 | G/A | D | G | D | G |

light, my strength, my song. This cor - ner - stone, this sol - id
God in help - less babe! This gift of love and right - eous -
world by dark - ness slain. Then burst - ing forth in glo - rious
pow'r of Christ in me. From life's first cry to fi - nal

| A | D/F# | G | D/F# | Em7 | G/A | D | D/F# |

ground, firm through the fierc - est drought and storm. What heights of
ness, scorned by the ones He came to save. Till on that
day, up from the grave He rose a - gain! And as He
breath, Je - sus com - mands my des - ti - ny. No pow'r of

| G | D/F# | A | D/F# | G | Bm7 |

love, what depths of peace, when fears are stilled, when striv - ings
cross as Je - sus died, the wrath of God was sat - is -
stands in vic - to - ry, sin's curse has lost its grip on
hell, no scheme of man, can ev - er pluck me from His

| A | G | D | G | A | D/F# |

cease! My Com - for - ter, my All in All, here in the
fied. For ev - 'ry sin on Him was laid; here in the
me, for I am His and He is mine, bought with the
hand. Till He re - turns or calls me home, here in the

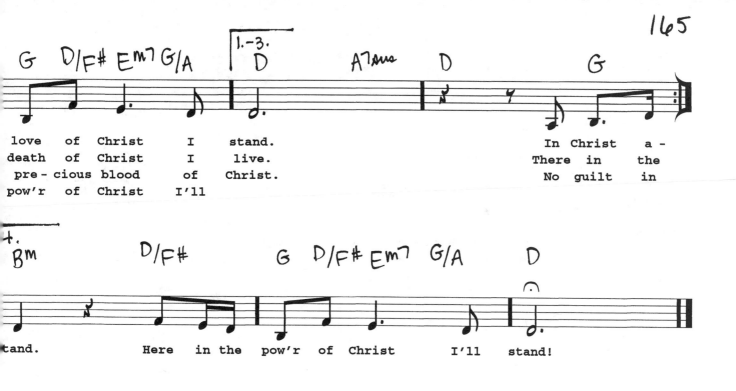

love   of Christ   I   stand.
death   of Christ   I   live.
pre - cious blood   of Christ.
pow'r   of Christ   I'll

In Christ a -
There in   the
No guilt   in

tand.   Here   in   the   pow'r   of   Christ   I'll   stand!

IT IS YOU

— Peter Furler

As we lift up our hands, __ will You meet us here?

As we call on Your name, __ will You meet us here?.

We have come to this place __ to wor-ship You, __

God of mer-cy and grace. __ It is You __ we a-dore.

It is You __ prais-es are for, __ on-ly You.

The heav-ens de-clare __ it is You, __ it is You..

And ho-ly, ho-ly is our God Al-might - y, __

170

JESUS, ALL FOR JESUS

— Robin Mark / Jennifer Atkinson

(MID.)

on - ly in   Your will__ that__ I   am

free.   Je - sus,   all   for

Je - sus,   all I   am   and have

and ev - er hope to   be.

JESUS, DRAW ME CLOSE

— Rick Founds

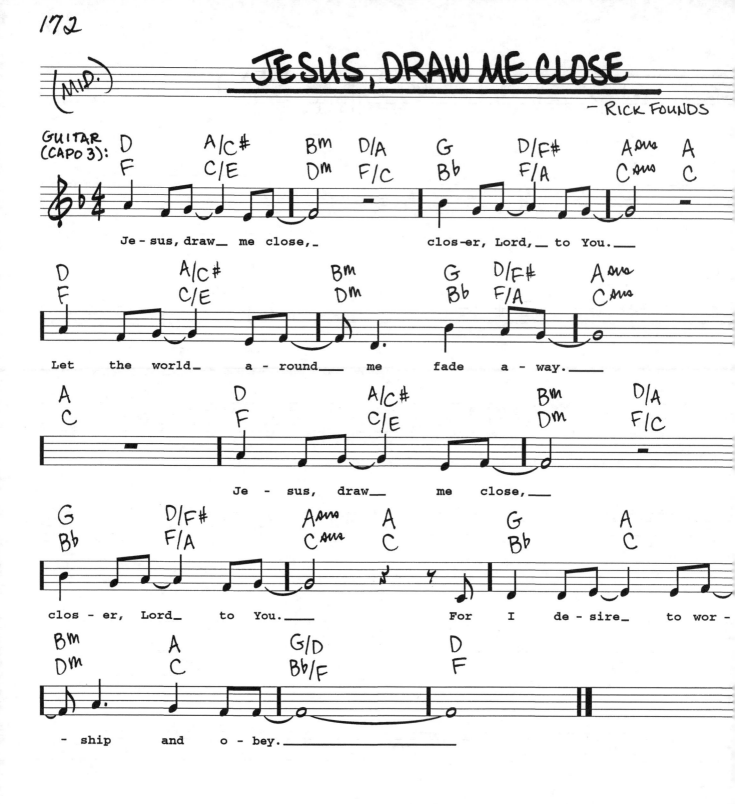

JESUS, LOVER OF MY SOUL

(SLOW/MID.)

— John Ezzy / Daniel Grul / Stephen McPherson

174

(MID/UP)

JESUS LORD OF HEAVEN
— PHIL WICKHAM

Je-sus, Lord of heav-en, I do not de-serve
Lord, I stand in won-der at the sac-ri-fice You made.

the grace that You have giv-en, or the
With mer-cy be-yond meas-ure, my debt

prom-ise of Your Word.
You free-ly paid. Your love is deep-

-er than an-y o-cean, high-er

than the heav-ens, reach-es be-yond the stars in the sky.

Je-sus, Your love has no bounds.

F ... **Am** ... **G** ... **F**

Je-sus, Your love has__ no bounds._____ Je-sus,

Am ... **G** ... **F** ... **Am** ... **G**

Your love has__ no bounds._ Je-sus, Your love has__ no bounds._

F ... **C** ... **G**

__ Your love is deep - er_____ than an-y o - cean,

Am ... **F** ... **C**

high - er than the heav - ens, reach - es_____

G ... **Am** ... **F**

be-yond the stars in the sky._____ Je-sus,

Am ... **G** ... **F**

Your love has__ no bounds.__

C
G/B
- en, Je-sus, Mes-si - ah,
Dsus
G
To ⊕
1.
2.
Lord of all. His All our hope
Am7
G/B
C
is in You, all our hope is in You.
Dsus
Am7
G/B
All the glo - ry to You, God,
C
Dsus
D.S. AL ⊕
the Light of the world. Je-sus, Mes-si -
Em7
G/D
Dsus
Je-sus, Mes-si - ah, Lord of all.
C
You're the Lord of all,
the Lord of all.
G

THE JOY OF THE LORD

—TWILA PARIS

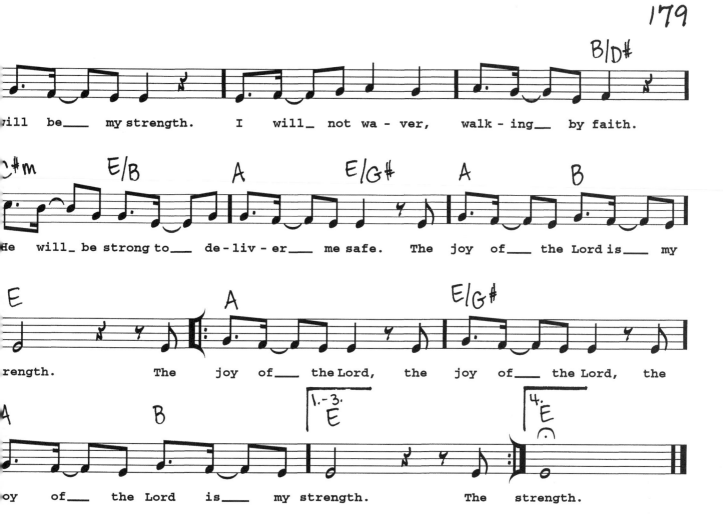

will be___ my strength. I will_ not wa - ver, walk - ing___ by faith.

He will_ be strong to___ de - liv - er___ me safe. The joy of___ the Lord is___ my

rength. The joy of___ the Lord, the joy of___ the Lord, the

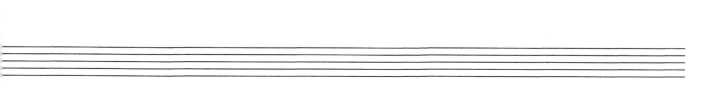

oy of___ the Lord is___ my strength. The strength.

King of Majesty

— Marty Sampson

182

(SLOW/MID.)

Lead Me To The Cross

— Brooke Fraser

Sav-ior, I come.___ I qui-et my soul,___
You were, as I,___ tempt-ed and tried,

re-mem-ber___ re-demp-tion's hill
hu-man.___ Word be-came flesh

___ where Your blood was spilled___ for my ran - som.___
___ bore my sin and death.___ Now You're ris - en.___}

And ev-'ry-thing___ I once___ held dear,___ I count

___ it all___ as loss.___ Lead me to the cross

where Your love poured___ out.___ Bring me to my knee

Lord, I lay me___ down.___ Rid me of___ my-self

Let Everything That Has Breath

— Matt Redman

186

Let God__ a - rise._____

Our__ God reigns__ now and for-ev - er, He reigns__

1. now and for-ev - er.

2. His__ en - - er.____

His__ en - - er.____

LET IT RISE

Holland Davis

LET MY WORDS BE FEW
(I'LL STAND IN AWE OF YOU)

(SLOW/MID)

— Matt Redman / Beth Redman

190

LET THE CHURCH RISE

(SLOW)

Israel Houghton / Jonathan Stockstill

We are a-live,__ filled with Your glo-rious__ life.
Mov-ing with pow'r,__ bring-ing Your name to the earth.

Out of the dark,__ in-to Your mar-v'lous__
Sing-ing Your prais-es, lift-ing up glo-rious__

light.
songs.
We are
We are

wait - ing with ex - pec - ta - tions.
mov - ing with His com - pas - sion.

Spir - it, raise us up with
Spir - it, fill our hearts with

You.}
You.}

And let the Church rise__ from the ash - es,__ let the Church

fall__ to her knees.__ Let us be light__ in the dark -

(MID./UP) LORD, I LIFT YOUR NAME ON HIGH

—RICK FOUNDS

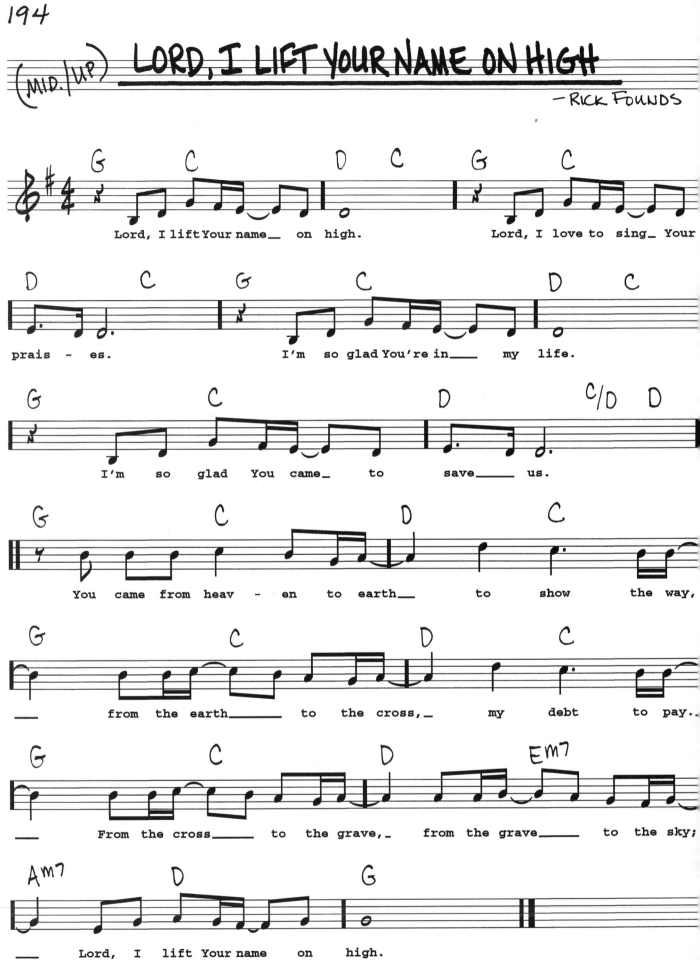

LORD, YOU HAVE MY HEART

—Martin Smith

Lord, You have my heart, and I will search for Yours.

Je-sus, take my life and lead me
Let me be to You a sac-ri-

on.
fice.

And I will raise You, Lord.

And I will sing of love come down.

And as You show Your grace,

we'll see Your glo-ry here.

LOVE THE LORD

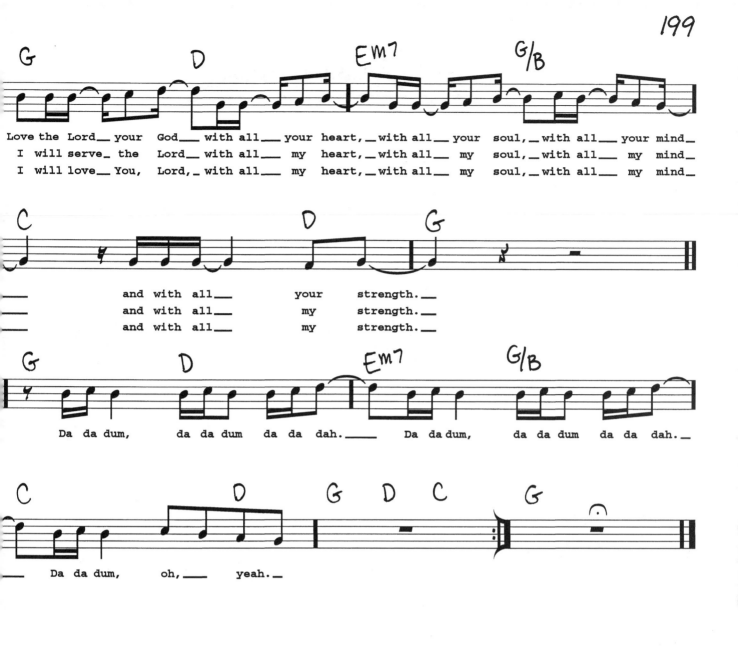

Love the Lord__ your God__ with all__ your heart, __with all__ your soul, __with all__ your mind__

I will serve_ the Lord__ with all__ my heart, __with all__ my soul, __with all__ my mind__

I will love__ You, Lord, _ with all__ my heart, __with all__ my soul, __with all__ my mind__

__ and with all__ your strength.__

__ and with all__ my strength.__

__ and with all__ my strength.__

Da da dum, da da dum da da dah.____ Da da dum, da da dum da da dah.__

__ Da da dum, oh, ___ yeah.__

Made to Worship

- Chris Tomlin / Ed Cash / Stephan Sharp

MAJESTIC

—Lincoln Brewster

The More I Seek You

-Zach Neese

208

Marvelous Light

— Charlie Hall

In-to mar-vel-ous light I'm run-ning, out of dark-ness,

out of shame. Through the cross You are the truth, You

are the life, You are the way. I once was fa-ther-less,

a stran-ger_ with no hope. Your kind-ness wak-ened me,

wak-ened me from my sleep. Your love, it
My dead heart

beck-ons deep-ly, a call to___ come and die.
now is beat-ing, my deep-est___ stain's now clean.

By grace now I will come and take this life, take Your life.}
Your breath fills up my lungs; now I'm free, now I'm free.}

Sin has lost its pow-er, death has lost its sting.

209

210

D   G   2. G

It's a mir - a - cle___ to me, ___

D/F#   G

(it's a mir - a - cle___ to me,) ___   and it's still a mys - ter - y, ___

D/F#   G

(and it's still a mys - ter - y.)   It's a mir - a - cle___   to me, ___

D/F#   EM7   A/C# D.S. AL ⊕

the pow - er___ of God___   for those who_ be - lieve. ___

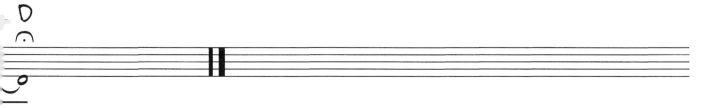

D

More Precious Than Silver

— Lynn DeShazo

New Doxology

— Genevan Psalter/Thomas Ken/Thomas Miller

Praise God, from whom all bless-ings flow. Praise
(Let) earth and heav'n-ly saints pro - claim the
(Praise) to the King, His throne tran - scends. His

Him, all crea-tures here be - low. Praise
pow'r and might of His great name. Let
crown and King-dom nev - er end. Now

Him a - bove, ye heav'n-ly hosts. Praise
us ex - alt on bend - ed knee. Praise
and through - out e - ter - ni - ty, I'll

Fa - ther, Son and Ho - ly Ghost.
God, the Ho - ly Trin - i - ty.
raise the One Who died for me.

Let Praise God, praise God, praise

God, Who saved my soul. Praise God, praise God, praise

God, from whom all bless-ings flow. Praise

flow.

218

MY REDEEMER LIVES

Reuben Morgan

220

MY SAVIOR LIVES

-Jon Egan/Glenn Packiam

(UP)

MY SAVIOR MY GOD

Aaron Shust

I am not skilled to un - der - stand
(I take Him at His word and) deed.
(Yes, liv - ing, dy - ing, let me) bring

what God has willed, what God has planned.
Christ died to save me, this I read,
my strength, my sol - ace from this spring,

I on - ly know at His right hand
and in my heart I find a need
that He who lives to be my King

stands One who is my Sav - ior.
of Him to be my Sav - ior.
once died to be my Sav - ior.

1.
I take Him at His word and

2., 3.
That He would leave His place on

high

and come for sin - ful men to___ die;

A New Hallelujah

Paul Baloche / Michael W. Smith / Debbie Smith

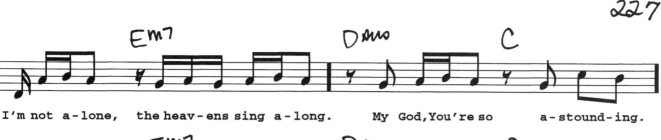

I'm not a-lone, the heav-ens sing a-long. My God, You're so a-stound-ing.

How could You be so good to me? E-ter-nal-ly, I be-lieve.

There is no one like You. There has nev - er

ev - er been an-y-one like You.

How could You be so good to me?

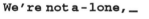

We're not a-lone,_ so sing a-long._ We're not a-lone,_

so sing a-long,_ sing a - long,_ sing a-long._

There is no one like You. There has nev - er

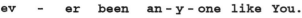

ev - er been an-y-one like You.

No Sweeter Name

- KARI JOBE

now I live___ to bring Him praise. And all my de-light___ is in___ You, Lord,___ all of my___ hope___ and all of my___ strength.. 'Cause all my de-light___ is in___ You, Lord,___ for-ev-er-more.___ to bring Him praise.

234

NOTHING BUT THE BLOOD

– Matt Redman

Your blood____ speaks a bet - ter word____ than all the emp - ty claims,
(Your cross)___ tes - ti - fies_ in grace,_ tells of the Fa - ther's heart_

I've heard up - on___ this earth,_ speaks right - eous - ness_ for me,___
to make a way_ for us.___ Now bold - ly we___ ap - proach,

and stands in my___ de - fense;_ Je - sus, it's_ Your blood.
not earth - ly con - fi - dence;_ it's on - ly by___ Your blood.

What can wash___ a - way___

____ our sins?_ What can make_ us whole___ a - gain?_

Noth - ing but the blood,____ noth - ing but the blood_ of Je - sus.

What can wash__ us pure__ as snow,__

wel-comed as__ the friends_ of God?__ Noth-ing but Your blood, __

noth-ing but Your blood,_King Je - sus. Your cross __

236

O CHURCH ARISE

(Slow/Mid.)

—Keith Getty / Stuart Townend

O Church, a- rise, and put your ar- mor on. Hear the
(Our call to) war: to love the cap- tive soul, but to
(Come see the) cross, where love and mer- cy meet, as the
(So Spir- it,) come, put strength in ev- 'ry stride. Give

call of Christ, our Cap- tain. For now the weak can say that
rage a- gainst the cap- tor. And with the sword that makes the
Son of God is strick- en. Then see His foes lie crushed be-
grace for ev- 'ry hur- dle, that we may run with faith to

they are strong in the strength that God has giv- en. With shield of
wound- ed whole, we will fight with faith and val- or. When faced with
neath His feet, for the Con- quer- or has ris- en. And as the
win the prize of a ser- vant good and faith- ful. As saints of

faith and belt of truth, we'll stand a- gainst the dev- il's
trials on ev- 'ry side, we know the out- come is se-
stone is rolled a- way, and Christ e- merg- es from the
old still line the way, re- tell- ing tri- umphs of His

lies, an ar- my bold, whose bat- tle cry is love, reach- ing
cure, and Christ will have the prize for which He died: an in-
grave, this vic- t'ry march con- tin- ues 'til the day ev- 'ry
grace, we hear their calls and hun- ger for the day when with

out to those in dark- ness.
her- i- tance of na- tions.   Our call to
eye and heart shall see Him.   Come see the
Christ we stand in glo- ry.   So Spir- it,

OH HOW HE LOVES YOU AND ME

-KURT KAISER

Oh, how He loves you and me! ___
Je-sus to Cal-v'ry did go, ___

Oh, how He loves you and me! ___
His love for sin-ners to show. ___

He gave His life; what___ more could He give?
What He did there brought___ hope from de-spair.

Oh, how He loves you. Oh, how He loves me.

Oh, how He loves you and me! ___

240

OFFERING

— Paul Baloche

No one on earth__ de-serves__ the prais - es that__ I sing.__

Je-sus, may You___ re-ceive__ the hon - or that__ You're due.__

O Lord,__ I bring__ an of - fer-ing__ to You.__

242

On The Third Day

— MARC BYRD / MATT MAHER

The win-ter's / And so we

On the third day,_ be-hold_ / On the third day,_ the saints_

the King._ On the third day,_ death has_ no sting._ On the / re - joice._ On the third day,_ we lift_ our voice._ On the

third day,_ we're for-giv-en and rec - on - ciled._ / third day,_ we're u - nit-ed and glo - ri - fied._

The earth, it

D.S. AL ⊕
(TAKE REPEAT)

ONCE AGAIN

— Matt Redman

(MID.)

Je - sus Christ, __ I think up - on Your sac - ri - fice.
Now You are __ ex - alt - ed to the high-est place,

You be - came noth - ing, poured out to death.
King of the heav - ens, where one day I'll bow. __

Man - y times __ I've won-dered at Your gift of life and
But for now, __ I mar - vel at this sav - ing grace and

I'm in that place __ once a - gain. __
I'm full of praise __ once a - gain. __

I'm in that place __ once a - gain. __
I'm full of praise __ once a - gain. __

Once a - gain I look up - on the cross where You died. __ I'm

hum - bled by Your mer - cy and I'm bro - ken in - side. __

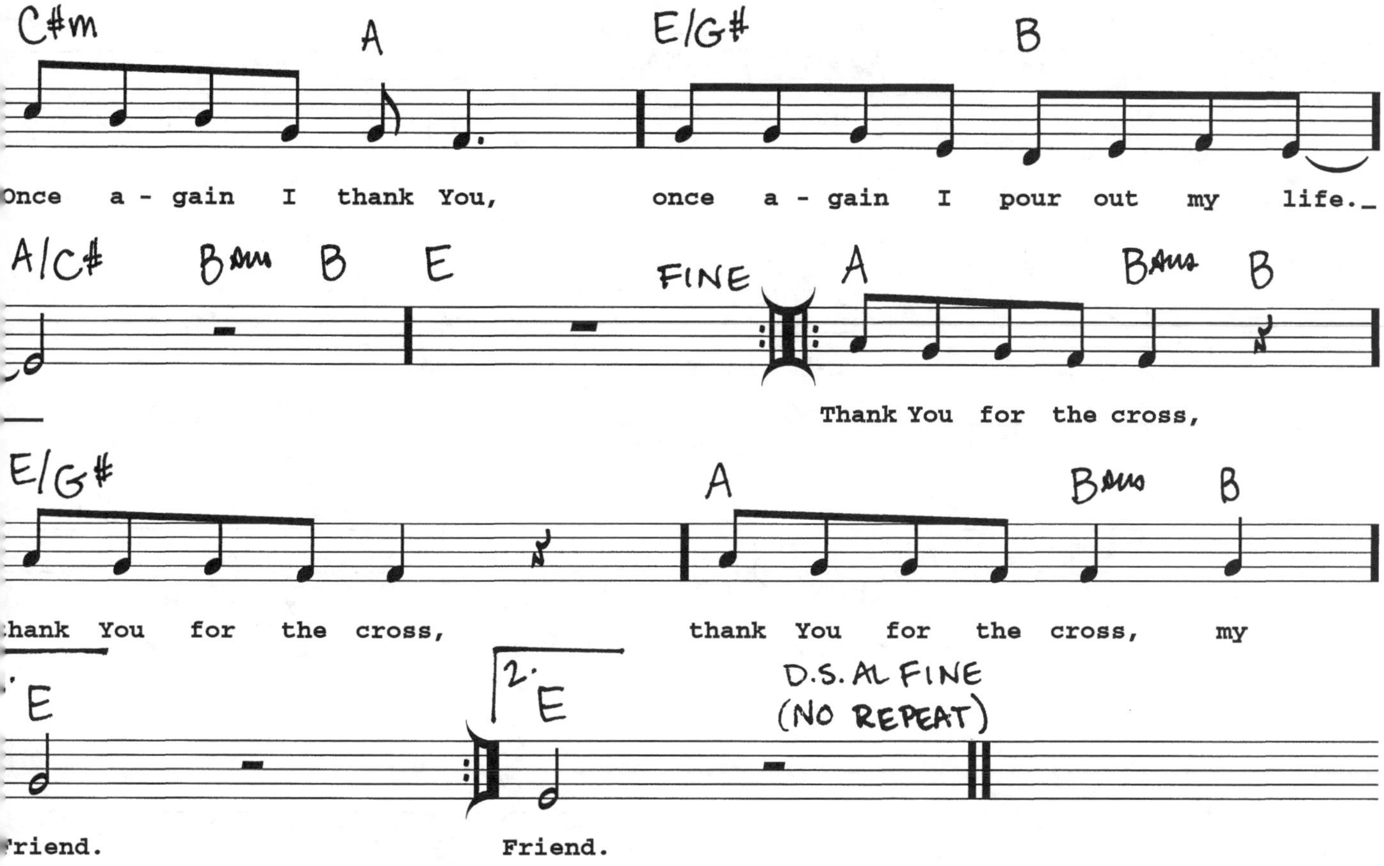

One Way

Joel Houston / Jonathon Douglass

I lay my life down at Your feet.
You're the only
You are al-ways, al-ways there, ev-'ry "how" and

One I need.
I turn to You and You___ are al-ways there.
ev-'ry "where." Your grace a-bounds so deep - ly with-in me.___

In trou-bled times, it's
So You will nev - er,

You I seek.
I put You first; that's all I need.
ev - er change; yes-ter-day, to - day the same,

I hum-ble all I am,___ all___ to You.___
for-ev-er 'til for-ev - er meets___ no end.___

One way: Je - sus.

You're the on - ly One that I could live for. One way:

(up)

OPEN THE EYES OF MY HEART

— PAUL BALOCHE

O - pen the eyes of my heart, Lord,

o - pen the eyes of my heart. I want to

see You, I want to see You.

1., 3.
D.C.

2., 4.

To see You high and lift - ed up,

shin - ing in the light of Your glo -

- ry. Pour out Your pow'r and love

1ST X D.C.
(TAKE REPEA

as we sing ho - ly, ho - ly, ho - ly.

hope in Your name.

Mourn - ing turns to songs of

praise. Our God saves,

Our God saves, our God saves.

252

jah!   Glo - ry   be   to__   our   great__   God!__   Hal - le -

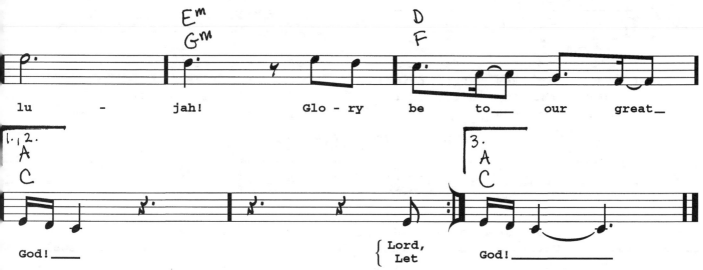

lu   -   jah!   Glo - ry   be   to__   our   great__

God!__   { Lord, God!_____
                Let

REDEEMER, SAVIOR, FRIEND

(SLOW)

— Darrell Evans/Chris Springer

PROMISES

—JARED ANDERSON

RESCUE

—JARED ANDERSON

Fmaj7　　　　　　Am　Em　Fmaj7　　　　Am　　　　　Em

I will fol-low You.＿　　　　　　　This world has noth-ing for＿

Fmaj7　　　　　　　　　Am　　　　　　　Em

＿ me.＿　　　　　This world has noth-ing　　for＿

Fmaj7　　　　　　　2. Fmaj7　　　　　　　　D.S. AL ⊕

＿ me.＿　　　　　　　＿ me.＿　　I　need You,　Je -

F　　　　　　Dm7　　　　　　　　　F

＿　Won't You cap - ture me＿ with　grace?＿　　Cap -

Dm7　　　　　　　　F　　　　　　　C

- ture　me＿ with　grace.＿　I will fol-low　You.＿

REVELATION SONG

— JENNIE LEE RIDDLE

(SLOW)

Revival

Robin Mark

264

RISE UP AND PRAISE HIM

— Paul Baloche / Gary Sadler

Let the heav-ens re-joice,___ let the earth__ be__ glad.

Let the peo-ple of God____ sing__ His__ praise.

__ all o-ver the land.__ Ev-'ry-one in the val-

- ley,_ come and lift_ your_ voice.__

All those_ on the moun - tain - top,_ be__ glad and shout_ for joy!

__ Rise up___ and praise___ Him,

He de-serves__ our__ love.__ Rise up___ and praise

Him, wor-ship the Ho - ly

One with all your heart, with all your soul, with all your might..

Rise up and praise Him!

Let the heav-ens re-joice._

SALT AND LIGHT

-Jan L'Ecuyer / John L'Ecuyer

SALVATION IS HERE

—JOEL HOUSTON

SHINE, JESUS, SHINE

—Graham Kendrick

Lord, the light of Your love is shin - ing, in the midst of the
Lord, I come to Your awe - some pres - ence, from the shad - ows in -
As we gaze on Your king - ly bright - ness, so our fac - es dis -

ark - ness shin - ing. Je - sus, Light of the world, shine up - on us,
to Your ra - diance. By the blood I may en - ter Your bright - ness;
lay Your like - ness. Ev - er chang - ing from glo - ry to glo - ry,

set us free by the truth You now bring us.
arch me, try me, con - sume all my dark - ness. } Shine on
ir - rored here, may our lives tell Your sto - ry.

me, shine on me. Shine, Je - sus, shine;

fill this land with the Fa - ther's glo - ry. Blaze, Spir - it, blaze;

set our hearts on fire.

low, riv - er, flow; flood the na - tions with grace and mer - cy.

end forth Your Word, Lord, and let there be light.

270

SAVIOUR KING

— MARTY SAMPSON/MIA FIELDES

(SLOW/MID.)

Say So

— Michael Gungor / Israel Houghton

SHINE

– MATT REDMAN

275

SHOUT TO THE LORD

—DARLENE ZSCHECH

SHOUT TO THE NORTH

— Martin Smith

(SLOW/MID.)

Men of faith, rise up and sing of the
(Rise up,) wom-en of the truth; stand and
(Rise up,) church with bro-ken wings; fill this

great and glo-rious King. You are strong when you feel
sing to bro-ken hearts who can know the heal-ing
place with songs a-gain of our God who reigns on

weak; in your bro-ken-ness, com-plete.
pow'r of our awe-some King of love.
high. By His grace, a-gain we'll fly.

Shout to the north and the south,

sing to the east and the west. Je-sus is

Sav-ior to all, Lord of heav-en and earth.

Rise up, earth.

Sing For Joy

Lamont Hiebert

If we call___ to Him, He will an - swer us.
Draw___ near___ to Him, He is here___ with us.

If we run___ to Him, He will run___ to us.
Give___ Him___ your love, He's in love___ with us.

If we lift___ our hands, He will lift___ us up.
He will heal___ our hearts, He will cleanse_ our hands.

Come now, praise_ His name, all you saints_ of God.___
If we rend___ our hearts, He will heal___ our land.___

Oh, sing for joy to God, our strength. Oh, sing for joy to God, our strength, our strength.

Speak O Lord

Stuart Townend / Keith Getty

(SLOW)

Sing, Sing, Sing

—Chris Tomlin/Jesse Reeves/Daniel Carson/Travis Nunn/Matt Gilder

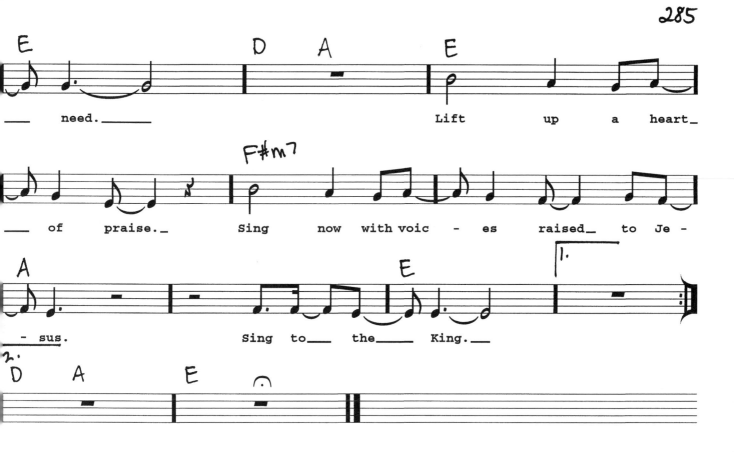

need._____ Lift up a heart_

_ of praise._ Sing now with voic - es raised_ to Je -

- sus. Sing to__ the__ King._

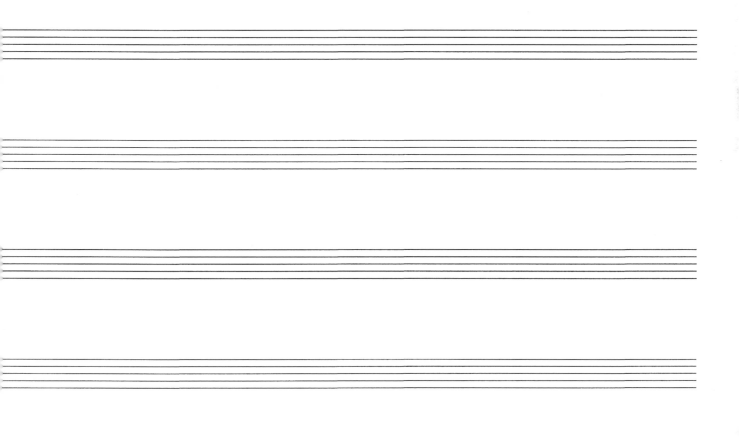

286

SON OF GOD

-TIM NEUFELD/JON NEUFELD/ED CASH/GORDON COCHRAN

(MID.)

290

(MID/UP)

Step By Step

—David Strasser "Beaker

O God, You are my___ God, and I will ev-er praise___ You. O God, You are my___ God, and I will ev-er praise___ You. I will seek You in the morn - ing, and I will learn to walk in Your___ ways._____ And step by step You'll lead___ me, and I will fol-low You all of my___ days.

STILL

—Reuben Morgan

(Slow)

Hide me now under Your wings..
rest, my soul, in Christ a - lone.

Cov - er me with -
Know His pow'r with - in

in Your might - y hand.
qui - et - ness and trust.

When the o-ceans rise and thun - ders roar,

I will soar with You a - bove the storm. Fa-ther, You are

King o - ver the flood. I will be still and know You are God.

Find

292

296

Take Me In

— Dave Browning

(MID.)

Take me past the out-er courts, __ in-to the ho-ly place, __ past the bra-zen al-tar; Lord, I want to see__ Your face. Pass me by the crowds__ of peo-ple, the priests who sing__ Your praise.__ I hun-ger and thirst__ for Your right-eous-ness,__ but it's on-ly found__ one place. Take me in to the Ho - ly of Ho - lies, take me in by the blood__ of__ the Lamb. __ Take me in to the Ho - ly of Ho - lies. Take the coal, __ cleanse my lips; here I am._____

THERE IS A REDEEMER

— MELODY GREEN

(MID.)

300

Thank You, Lord

— Paul Baloche / Don Moen

302

There Is A Higher Throne

– Keith Getty / Kristyn Lennox Getty

304

THERE IS JOY IN THE LORD

— Cheri Keaggy

(U.P.)

There is joy in the Lord, there is love in His Spir-it, there is hope in the knowl-edge of Him.

(1.,2.) There's a foun-tain I know; ev-'ry time I am near it, my heart o-ver-flows to the Lord.

(3.) There's a foun-tain that flows like a riv-er from heav-en, a-bound-ing in love to my soul.

All bless-ing and hon-or are His, all

glo - ry___ and pow - er___ are___ His.

Let all wis - dom___ and strength_ be the

rd's in___ this place.___ Let all glo - ry___ be

giv - en___ to Him. There is

It's a - bound - ing___ in love to___ my___

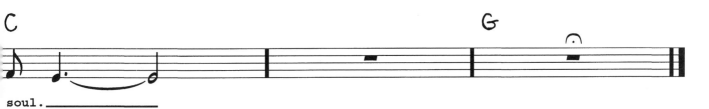

soul._____

306

'Til I See You

-Joel Houston / Jadwin Gillies

The great - est love_____ that an - y - one_ could ev - er know
_____ I'll live_ to see_ Your king - dom com
_____ that calls_the u - ni - verse_ to be,

that o - ver came_ the cross_ and grave_ to find_ my sou
and in my heart_ I pray_You'll let_ Your will_ be don
You are the whis - per in_____ my heart_that speaks_ to me.

And 'til I see_____ You face_ to face_ and grace a-maz

- ing takes_ me home,_ I'll trust in_____ You.

With all I am,_____ I will live_____ to lo

_____ You, I will live_____ to bring_ You praise._ I will liv

D.S. Al
(TAKE 2nd ENDIN

a child_ in awe_ of You._____ You are the voi

308

312

Yeah, we raise___ up ho - ly___ hands___

to praise___ the Ho - ly One___ who was___

and___ is___ and is___ to come.___

You were,_ You are,___

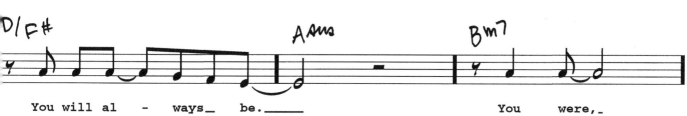

You will al - ways_ be.___ You were,_

You are,_ You will al - ways_ be.___ So, we___ raise_

314

UNDIGNIFIED

(MID/UP)

— MATT REDMAN

I will dance, I will sing, to be mad for my King.

Noth-ing, Lord, is hin-der-ing the pas-sion in my soul.

pas-sion in my soul. And I'll be-come

e-ven more un-dig-ni-fied than this.

Some would say it's fool-ish-ness, but I'll be-come

e-ven more un-dig-ni-fied than this.

Leave my pride by my side, and I'll be-come

e - ven more un - dig - ni - fied than this, than this.

La la la___ la la, hey! La la la___ la la, hey!

La la la___ la la, hey! La la la___ la la, hey!

La la la___ la la, hey! La la la___ la la, hey!

La la la___ la la. It's all for You, my Lord!

Unfailing Love

– Chris Tomlin / Ed Cash / Cary Pierce

(Slow / Mid.)

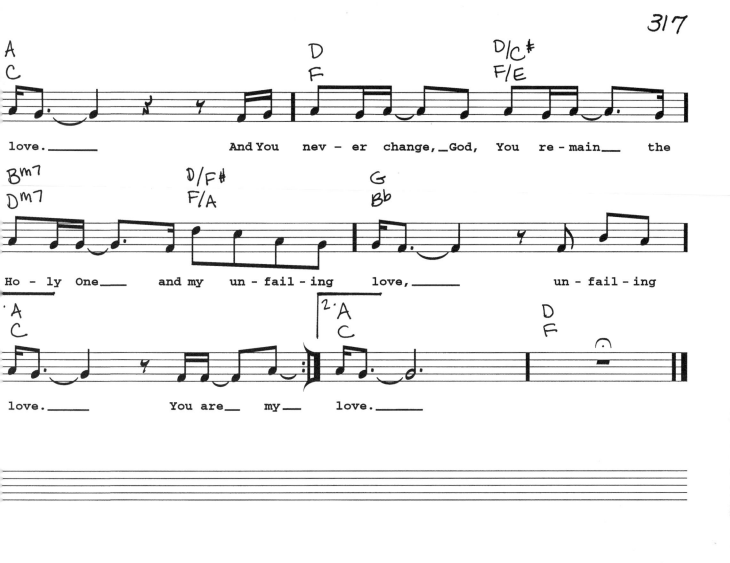

love._____ And You nev - er change,__God, You re - main__ the

Ho - ly One___ and my un - fail - ing love,_____ un - fail - ing

love._____ You are__ my__ love._____

318

WE GIVE YOU GLORY

—Jeremy Camp

We have raised a thou - sand voic - es, just to
(As we) fall down be - fore You, with our

lift Your ho - ly name,___ and we will raise thou - sands more
will - ing hearts we seek.___ In the great-ness of___ Your___ glo -

___ to sing___ of Your beau - ty in___ this place.___ Well,___
- ry,___ it's so hard to e - ven speak.___ There is

none can e - ven___ fath - om, no, not one de - fine___ Your worth
noth - ing we___ can___ of - fer, no,___ noth - ing can___ re - pay.

as we mar - vel in___ Your___ pres - ence to the
So we give You all___ our___ prais - es and

ends of___ the earth.___
lift our voice___ to sing.___ } We give You glo - ry.___

Lift-in' up our hands and sing-in' Ho - ly.___ You a - lone___ are

WE WANT TO SEE JESUS LIFTED HIGH

-Doug Horley

We want to see Je - sus lift - ed high,

a ban - ner that flies___ a - cross___ this land,

that all men might see___ the truth___ and know.

He is the way___ to heav - en. We want to see,

we want to see, we want to see Je -

- sus lift - ed high.___ We want to see, we want to see,

we want to see Je - sus lift - ed high.___ Step by

322

WE WILL WORSHIP HIM

—BRENTON BROWN

(MID.)

Let us come____ to-geth-er, let us join as one,__ let us
(It is time)____ for bat-tle, it is time for war,__ as we

turn our fac-es to the ris-ing sun.__ Let us
sing ho-san-na, as we praise the Lord.__ He will

go up to Zi-on, to God's ho-ly hill,__ a might-y ar-
still the ac-cus-er, crush the en-e-my,__ as we cel-

-my that__ will wor-ship Him.⎫
-e-brate_ God's vic-to-ry.⎭   We will wor-ship

Him,   we will wor-ship Him.   Je-sus, He's__ our

King.   We will wor-ship Him.___   Let the o-ceans

roar,_____ let the heav-ens ring   to the glo-ry of___ our

God as we wor-ship Him.   It is time_ Him.

WHAT CAN I DO?

(SLOW/MID.)

– PAUL BALOCHE / GRAHAM KENDRICK

When I see the beau - ty of a sun-set's glo - ry, a - maz - ing
(When I hear the) sto - ry of a God of mer - cy, who shared hu -

art - ist - ry a-cross the eve - ning sky, when I feel the mys-ter - y of a dis-tant
man - i - ty and suf-fered by___ our side, of the cross they nailed You to, but could not

gal - ax - y, it awes and hum - bles___ me___ to be
hold___ You; now You're mak - ing all things___ new___ by the

loved by a God so___ high.}
pow'r of Your ris - en___ life.} What can I do but thank You?

What can I do but give my life to You?___ Hal-le-lu - jah! Hal-le-lu-jah! What can I

do but praise You ev-er-y day___ with ev-'ry-thing I do?___ Hal-le-lu - jah!

Hal-le-lu - jah!___ Hal-le-lu - jah! When I hear the jah!

324

When It's All Been Said and Done

(Slow/Mid.)

– James A. Cowan

328

THE WONDERFUL CROSS

- Jesse Reeves / Chris Tomlin / J.D. Walt

When I sur-vey the___ won-drous___ cross
See from His head, His___ hands, His___ feet,
Were the whole realm of___ na-ture___ mine,

on which the Prince of_____ Glo-ry___ died,
sor-row and love flow_____ min-gled___ down.
that were an of-f'ring_____ far too___ small.

my rich-est gain I_____ count but___ loss,
Did e'er such love and___ sor-row___ meet,
Love so a-maz-ing,___ so di-vine,

and pour con-tempt on all my_____ pride.
or thorns com-pose so rich a_____
de-mands my soul, my life, my_____

crown? } O the won-der-ful cross,___ O the won-der-ful cross
all. }

___ bids___ me come___ and die___ and find___ that___ I___ may tru-

WONDERFUL MAKER

- Matt Redman / Chris Tomlin

(SLOW/MID.)

You spread out the skies o-ver emp-ty space, said, "Let there be light;" to a

dark and form-less world Your light was born.

You spread out Your arms o-ver emp-ty hearts, said, "Let there be light;" to a
eye has ful-ly seen how beau-ti-ful the cross, and we have on-ly heard the__

dark and hope-less world Your Son was born.
faint-est whis-pers of how great You are.

You

made the world and saw that it was good. You sent Your on-ly Son, for You are__

__ good.____ What a won-der-ful Mak - er,____

what a won-der-ful Sav - ior._____ How ma-jes-tic Your whis-

332

Wonderful, Merciful Savior

-Dawn Rodgers / Eric Wyse

You are the One that we praise,___

You are the One we a - dore,___

You give the heal - ing and grace our

hearts al - ways hun - ger for, oh,___ our

hearts al - ways hun - ger for.___

334

WORTHY IS THE LAMB

- Darlene Zschech

(Slow/Mid.)

Thank You for the cross, Lord.___ Thank You for the price You paid.___ Bear-ing all my sin and_ shame,_ in love You_ came_ and gave a-maz-ing grace.__ Thank You for this love, Lord._____ Thank You for the nail - pierced hands._ Washed me in Your cleans-ing_ flow,_ now all I__ know,_ Your for-give - ness and__ em - brace.__ Wor - thy is__ the Lamb,_ seat - ed on__ the throne.__

r "Treasure"

336.

You Alone

-Jack Parker/David Crowder

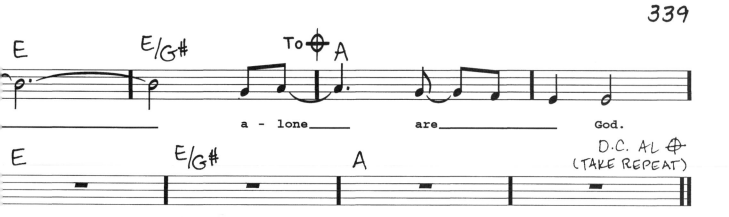

a - lone____ are_____ God.

D.C. AL ⊕
(TAKE REPEAT)

are__ God.

I'm a - live,__ I'm a - live,__

I'm a - live,__ I'm a - live. I'm a - live,__ I'm a - live,__

I'm a - live,__ I'm a - live. _____

You_____ a - lone____ are__ Fa - ther, and You__

a - lone____ are__ good.

You_____ a - lone____ are__ Sav - ior, and You__

a - lone____ are__ God.

340

You Are God Alone
(Not A God)

- Billy J. Foote / Cindy Foote

(Slow/Mid.)

You are not a god cre - at - ed
You're the on - ly God whose pow - er

by hu - man hands.
none can con - tend.
You are not a god de - pend -
You're the on - ly God whose name

- ent on an - y mor - tal man.
__ and praise will nev - er end.
You are not a
You're the on - ly

god in need_____ of_____ an - y - thing we can give.
God who's wor - thy_____ of ev - 'ry - thing we can give.

By Your plan, that's just the way__ it is.__
You are God, that's just the way__ it is.__

You are God__ a - lone.____ From be

fore time be - gan,____ You were on__ Your throne

342

You Are Good

Israel Houghton

YOUR NAME

Paul Baloche / Glenn Packiam

(Slow/Mid.)

348

You Gave Your Life Away

– Paul Baloche / Kathryn Scott

You spoke_ and worlds_ were formed,_ You breathed_ and life_ was born.
You lived_ a sin - less life,___ yet You___ were cru - ci - fied.

You knew___ that one_ day You_ would come.___
You bought_ our free - dom on_ the cross.___

So far_ from Heav - en's throne,_ clothed_ in hu - man form,_
For-sak - en for_ our sin,___ You died and rose_ a - gain.___

You showed_ the world_ the Fa - ther's love._ }
Je - sus,___ You are_ the Lamb_ of God.___ }

You gave,_

You gave_ Your life_ a-way. You gave,_ You gave_ Your life_ a-way. You gave,

You gave_ Your life_ a-way for_ me. Your grace

has bro - ken ev - 'ry chain, my sins___ are gone,_ my debt's_ been paid. You gave

352

You, You Are God

- Michael Walker Beach

Here I am; __ I've come to find __ You.
Here I am; __ I've come to thank __ You.

Here I am __ to see __ Your grace,
Here I am, __ a life __ You've changed

__ to bring to You __ an of-
Be - cause You gave __ Your life

- fer - ing. __ I have to ask __ my - self __ one thing: __
__ for me, __ You cru-ci - fied __ Your Son __ for me, __

How can I __ do an - y - thing __ but __ praise? __
how can I __ do an - y - thing __ but __ praise? __

__ I _____ praise. _____
__ I _____ praise. _____

You, You are God, __ You are Lord, __ You are all __

354

(MID./UP)

You're Worthy Of My Praise

-David Ruis

I will give__ You all my praise._____ You a-lone__ I

ong to wor - ship, You a-lone__ are wor - thy of__ my__

raise.

aise.

356

Your Grace Is Enough

- Matt Maher

Your Love Is Deep

-Dan Collins/Susanna Bussey Kirksey/Jami Smith

KEY INDEX

MAJOR KEYS

C MAJOR

ANCIENT OF DAYS 24

BE UNTO YOUR NAME 36

BETTER THAN LIFE 50

BLESS THE LORD 52

CAME TO MY RESCUE 58

EVERLASTING GOD 80

FROM THE INSIDE OUT 98

GREAT IS THE LORD 118

HAPPY DAY 120

HEAR OUR PRAISES 122

HEAR US FROM HEAVEN 124

I WILL CALL UPON THE LORD 160

IT IS YOU 168

JESUS LORD OF HEAVEN 174

MADE ME GLAD 200

MAJESTY (HERE I AM) 206

NONE BUT JESUS 230

OUR GREAT GOD 252

THE POWER OF THE CROSS
      (OH TO SEE THE DAWN) 254

RESCUE 258

SPEAK O LORD 281

STILL 291

WHEN IT'S ALL BEEN SAID
      AND DONE 324

WONDERFUL, MERCIFUL SAVIOR 332

YOU ARE GOD ALONE (NOT A GOD) 340

D MAJOR

ALL WE NEED 20

AMAZED 19

AMAZING GRACE
      (MY CHAINS ARE GONE) 22

BE LIFTED HIGH 33

BEAUTIFUL ONE 38

BEAUTIFUL SAVIOR (ALL MY DAYS) 40

BEFORE THE THRONE OF GOD ABOVE 46

BLESSED 54

COME, NOW IS THE TIME TO WORSHIP 64

COME THOU FOUNT, COME THOU KING 66

DANCING GENERATION 72

EVERYTHING GLORIOUS 82

FAMOUS ONE 86

FOR WHO YOU ARE 92

FRIEND OF GOD 96

GOD IS GREAT 110

GRACE FLOWS DOWN 116

THE HEART OF WORSHIP 126

HERE I AM TO WORSHIP 128

HERE IN YOUR PRESENCE 130

HIDING PLACE 125

HOLY IS YOUR NAME 136

HOW DEEP THE FATHER'S
      LOVE FOR US 146

HOW HE LOVES 150

I AM FREE 152

I COULD SING OF YOUR
      LOVE FOREVER 154

I WILL BOAST 147

IN CHRIST ALONE 164

JESUS, ALL FOR JESUS 170

THE JOY OF THE LORD 178

LEAD ME TO THE CROSS 182

LET THE PRAISES RING 192

LORD, YOU HAVE MY HEART 195

MAJESTIC 204

MIGHTY IS THE POWER OF
      THE CROSS 210

THE MORE I SEEK YOU 205

MY SAVIOR MY GOD 222

O CHURCH ARISE 236

ON THE THIRD DAY 242

OPEN THE EYES OF MY HEART 248

D MAJOR (cont.)

OUR GOD SAVES.............................. 250

REDEEMER, SAVIOR, FRIEND 255

REVELATION SONG........................... 260

REVIVAL....................................... 262

RISE UP AND PRAISE HIM 264

STRONG TOWER 292

SWEETER...................................... 294

TAKE MY LIFE................................ 298

THERE IS A REDEEMER 297

TIL I SEE YOU 306

UNCHANGING................................. 312

UNDIGNIFIED 314

WE FALL DOWN 309

WE GIVE YOU GLORY 318

WE WILL WORSHIP HIM.................... 322

THE WONDERFUL CROSS 328

YESTERDAY, TODAY AND FOREVER....... 336

YOU ARE MY KING (AMAZING LOVE) ... 346

YOUR LOVE IS DEEP 358

E MAJOR

AGAIN I SAY REJOICE......................... 10

ARISE 28

AT THE CROSS 30

BETTER IS ONE DAY 48

CELEBRATE THE LORD OF LOVE 60

CENTER 62

COUNTING ON GOD........................... 70

FOR ALL YOU'VE DONE 90

FROM THE RISING............................. 100

HOSANNA 140

HOSANNA (PRAISE IS RISING) 142

I GIVE YOU MY HEART 156

I WILL EXALT YOUR NAME................. 161

LET EVERYTHING THAT HAS BREATH .. 184

MY REDEEMER LIVES........................ 218

A NEW HALLELUJAH........................... 224

ONCE AGAIN 244

SAVIOUR KING 270

SAY SO.. 272

SING FOR JOY 280

SING TO THE KING............................ 284

THERE IS A HIGHER THRONE 302

YOU ALONE 338

YOU ARE GOOD 342

F MAJOR (with capo chords)

ANCIENT WORDS................................. 26

EVERYTHING 61

HE IS EXALTED 103

HOLY SPIRIT RAIN DOWN.................... 138

JESUS, DRAW ME CLOSE...................... 172

MORE PRECIOUS THAN SILVER 214

OFFERING 240

THANK YOU, LORD............................ 300

UNFAILING LOVE............................... 316

G MAJOR

ABOVE ALL.. 8

AGNUS DEI...................................... 9

ALL BOW DOWN 16

ALL THE EARTH WILL SING
        YOUR PRAISES 18

AT THE FOOT OF THE CROSS................. 29

AWESOME GOD.................................. 32

AWESOME IS THE LORD MOST HIGH 34

BEAUTY OF THE LORD 42

BECAUSE OF YOUR LOVE...................... 44

BREATHE.. 43

CONSUMING FIRE.............................. 68

DAYS OF ELIJAH............................... 74

ENOUGH... 78

FACEDOWN...................................... 84

G MAJOR (cont.)

FILLED WITH YOUR GLORY 88

FOREVER 94

GIVE THANKS 102

GIVE US CLEAN HANDS 104

GLORY TO GOD FOREVER 108

GOD OF WONDERS 114

HERE IS OUR KING 132

HOLY IS THE LORD 134

HOW CAN I KEEP FROM SINGING 144

HOW GREAT IS OUR GOD 148

I KNOW WHO I AM 158

I WILL RISE 162

INDESCRIBABLE 166

JESUS, LOVER OF MY SOUL 173

JESUS MESSIAH 176

KING OF MAJESTY 180

LET GOD ARISE 186

LET IT RISE 188

LET MY WORDS BE FEW
      (I'LL STAND IN AWE OF YOU) 189

LET THE CHURCH RISE 190

LORD, I LIFT YOUR NAME ON HIGH 194

LORD, REIGN IN ME 196

LOVE THE LORD 198

MADE TO WORSHIP 202

MIGHTY TO SAVE 212

MY SAVIOR LIVES 220

NEW DOXOLOGY 215

NO ONE LIKE YOU 226

NO SWEETER NAME 228

NOT TO US 232

O PRAISE HIM
      (ALL THIS FOR A KING) 238

PROMISES 256

SALT AND LIGHT 266

SALVATION IS HERE 268

SHINE 274

SHOUT TO THE NORTH 278

SON OF GOD 286

STEP BY STEP 290

THERE IS JOY IN THE LORD 304

TO THE ONLY GOD 308

TODAY IS THE DAY 310

WE WANT TO SEE JESUS
      LIFTED HIGH 320

WHAT CAN I DO? 323

WHOLLY YOURS 326

WONDERFUL MAKER 330

WORTHY IS THE LAMB 334

YOU ARE MY ALL IN ALL 344

YOU GAVE YOUR LIFE AWAY 348

YOU'RE WORTHY OF MY PRAISE 354

YOUR GRACE IS ENOUGH 356

YOUR NAME 345

A MAJOR

ALL BECAUSE OF JESUS 14

BLESSED BE YOUR NAME 56

DRAW ME CLOSE 76

GLORY IN THE HIGHEST 106

MARVELOUS LIGHT 208

MY HOPE IS YOU 216

NOTHING BUT THE BLOOD 234

OH HOW HE LOVES YOU AND ME 237

ONE WAY 246

SHINE, JESUS, SHINE 269

THE STAND 288

YOU NEVER LET GO 350

YOU, YOU ARE GOD 352

B♭ MAJOR (with capo chords)

ALIVE FOREVER AMEN 12

GOD OF THIS CITY 112

SHOUT TO THE LORD 276

SING, SING, SING 282

MINOR KEYS

A MINOR

BLESS THE LORD 52

HEAR US FROM HEAVEN....................... 124

IT IS YOU... 168

MAJESTY (HERE I AM)........................ 206

RESCUE.. 258

B MINOR

BEAUTIFUL SAVIOR (ALL MY DAYS) 40

HIDING PLACE 125

LEAD ME TO THE CROSS..................... 182

LORD, YOU HAVE MY HEART 195

STRONG TOWER 292

YESTERDAY, TODAY AND FOREVER....... 336

E MINOR

AWESOME GOD...................................... 32

FACEDOWN.. 84

TAKE ME IN 296

G MINOR (with capo chords)

GOD OF THIS CITY 112

NOTE: Songs that begin in a minor key and
switch to the relative major key are
listed under both keys.

TEMPO INDEX

UP TEMPO (above 116 bpm)

AGAIN I SAY REJOICE........................... 10

ALL BECAUSE OF JESUS 14

ALL THE EARTH WILL SING
      YOUR PRAISES 18

ALL WE NEED.................................... 20

AWESOME IS THE LORD MOST HIGH 34

BEAUTIFUL ONE................................. 38

BECAUSE OF YOUR LOVE...................... 44

COUNTING ON GOD 70

DANCING GENERATION 72

EVERLASTING GOD 80

FILLED WITH YOUR GLORY 88

FOR ALL YOU'VE DONE 90

FOR WHO YOU ARE 92

FOREVER 94

FRIEND OF GOD 96

FROM THE RISING............................... 100

GOD IS GREAT................................... 110

HAPPY DAY 120

HEAR OUR PRAISES............................. 122

I AM FREE.. 152

I KNOW WHO I AM.............................. 158

I WILL BOAST 147

KING OF MAJESTY.............................. 180

LET EVERYTHING THAT HAS BREATH .. 184

LET GOD ARISE.................................. 186

LET THE PRAISES RING 192

MAJESTIC... 204

MARVELOUS LIGHT............................. 208

MY REDEEMER LIVES.......................... 218

MY SAVIOR LIVES............................... 220

NOT TO US 232

ONE WAY 246

OPEN THE EYES OF MY HEART 248

PROMISES... 256

REVIVAL... 262

RISE UP AND PRAISE HIM 264

SALT AND LIGHT 266

SALVATION IS HERE............................ 268

SAY SO... 272

SHINE, JESUS, SHINE 269

SING FOR JOY.................................... 280

SING, SING, SING 282

THERE IS JOY IN THE LORD 304

TODAY IS THE DAY 310

WE GIVE YOU GLORY 318

WE WANT TO SEE JESUS
      LIFTED HIGH........................... 320

YOU ARE GOOD 342

YOU, YOU ARE GOD 352

YOUR GRACE IS ENOUGH 356

MID/UP TEMPO (93-116 bpm)

ALIVE FOREVER AMEN.......................... 12

ALL BOW DOWN.................................. 16

ARISE 28

BLESSED BE YOUR NAME 56

CELEBRATE THE LORD OF LOVE 60

CENTER 62

COME, NOW IS THE TIME TO WORSHIP.... 64

DAYS OF ELIJAH................................. 74

GLORY TO GOD FOREVER 108

HERE IS OUR KING 132

HOLY IS YOUR NAME 136

HOSANNA (PRAISE IS RISING) 142

I WILL CALL UPON THE LORD............... 160

JESUS LORD OF HEAVEN...................... 174

LORD, I LIFT YOUR NAME ON HIGH 194

LORD, REIGN IN ME 196

LOVE THE LORD................................. 198

MY HOPE IS YOU 216

A NEW HALLELUJAH............................ 224

O PRAISE HIM
      (ALL THIS FOR A KING)............ 238

MID/UP TEMPO (cont.)

OUR GOD SAVES 250

SING TO THE KING....................... 284

STEP BY STEP.............................. 290

SWEETER...................................... 294

THANK YOU, LORD........................ 300

UNCHANGING............................... 312

UNDIGNIFIED 314

WONDERFUL, MERCIFUL SAVIOR.......... 332

YESTERDAY, TODAY AND FOREVER....... 336

YOU'RE WORTHY OF MY PRAISE.......... 354

MID TEMPO (77-92 bpm)

ANCIENT OF DAYS 24

AWESOME GOD.............................. 32

BETTER IS ONE DAY 48

BETTER THAN LIFE 50

BLESSED...................................... 54

CAME TO MY RESCUE 58

COME THOU FOUNT, COME THOU KING.... 66

ENOUGH....................................... 78

EVERYTHING GLORIOUS 82

GIVE THANKS 102

GLORY IN THE HIGHEST 106

GOD OF WONDERS......................... 114

HERE I AM TO WORSHIP 128

HOLY IS THE LORD 134

HOSANNA 140

I COULD SING OF YOUR
　　LOVE FOREVER 154

I WILL EXALT YOUR NAME.............. 161

I WILL RISE 162

IT IS YOU..................................... 168

JESUS, ALL FOR JESUS 170

JESUS, DRAW ME CLOSE 172

JESUS MESSIAH............................. 176

THE JOY OF THE LORD 178

LET IT RISE 188

LORD, YOU HAVE MY HEART 195

MADE ME GLAD 200

MADE TO WORSHIP........................ 202

MIGHTY TO SAVE.......................... 212

MORE PRECIOUS THAN SILVER 214

MY SAVIOR MY GOD 222

NEW DOXOLOGY........................... 215

NO ONE LIKE YOU 226

NOTHING BUT THE BLOOD 234

OH HOW HE LOVES YOU AND ME 237

ON THE THIRD DAY 242

ONCE AGAIN 244

RESCUE....................................... 258

SHINE 274

SHOUT TO THE LORD 276

SON OF GOD................................ 286

TAKE ME IN 296

TAKE MY LIFE.............................. 298

THERE IS A HIGHER THRONE 302

THERE IS A REDEEMER.................. 297

TIL I SEE YOU.............................. 306

WE WILL WORSHIP HIM................. 322

THE WONDERFUL CROSS................. 328

YOU ALONE.................................. 338

SLOW/MID TEMPO (68-76 bpm)

ABOVE ALL................................... 8

AGNUS DEI................................... 9

ANCIENT WORDS............................ 26

AT THE CROSS 30

AT THE FOOT OF THE CROSS............ 29

BE LIFTED HIGH 33

BE UNTO YOUR NAME.................... 36

BEFORE THE THRONE OF GOD ABOVE..... 46

CONSUMING FIRE........................... 68

SLOW/MID TEMPO (cont.)

DRAW ME CLOSE 76

FACEDOWN.. 84

FAMOUS ONE 86

FROM THE INSIDE OUT 98

GIVE US CLEAN HANDS 104

GOD OF THIS CITY 112

GRACE FLOWS DOWN 116

HEAR US FROM HEAVEN...................... 124

THE HEART OF WORSHIP..................... 126

HIDING PLACE 125

HOLY SPIRIT RAIN DOWN..................... 138

HOW CAN I KEEP FROM SINGING......... 144

HOW GREAT IS OUR GOD..................... 148

I GIVE YOU MY HEART 156

IN CHRIST ALONE 164

JESUS, LOVER OF MY SOUL.................. 173

LEAD ME TO THE CROSS...................... 182

LET MY WORDS BE FEW
    (I'LL STAND IN AWE OF YOU)..... 189

MAJESTY (HERE I AM)......................... 206

MIGHTY IS THE POWER OF
    THE CROSS.................................... 210

THE MORE I SEEK YOU........................ 205

NONE BUT JESUS 230

O CHURCH ARISE................................. 236

SAVIOUR KING 270

SHOUT TO THE NORTH 278

THE STAND.. 288

STRONG TOWER 292

UNFAILING LOVE................................... 316

WE FALL DOWN 309

WHAT CAN I DO? 323

WHEN IT'S ALL BEEN SAID
    AND DONE..................................... 324

WHOLLY YOURS 326

WONDERFUL MAKER 330

WORTHY IS THE LAMB 334

YOU ARE GOD ALONE (NOT A GOD)....... 340

YOU ARE MY ALL IN ALL 344

YOU ARE MY KING (AMAZING LOVE) ... 346

YOU NEVER LET GO 350

YOUR LOVE IS DEEP 358

YOUR NAME... 345

SLOW TEMPO (below 68 bpm)

AMAZED 19

AMAZING GRACE
    (MY CHAINS ARE GONE).............. 22

BEAUTIFUL SAVIOR (ALL MY DAYS) 40

BEAUTY OF THE LORD........................ 42

BLESS THE LORD 52

BREATHE... 43

EVERYTHING 61

GREAT IS THE LORD 118

HE IS EXALTED 103

HERE IN YOUR PRESENCE................... 130

HOW DEEP THE FATHER'S
    LOVE FOR US............................. 146

HOW HE LOVES 150

INDESCRIBABLE.................................... 166

LET THE CHURCH RISE........................ 190

NO SWEETER NAME.............................. 228

OFFERING 240

OUR GREAT GOD 252

THE POWER OF THE CROSS
    (OH TO SEE THE DAWN)............. 254

REDEEMER, SAVIOR, FRIEND 255

REVELATION SONG............................... 260

SPEAK O LORD 281

STILL... 291

TO THE ONLY GOD 308

YOU GAVE YOUR LIFE AWAY 348

MORE WORSHIP RESOURCES

WORSHIP BAND PLAY-ALONG SERIES

(Available for Guitar, Keyboard, Bass, Drumset, and Vocal)

Volume 1 – Holy Is the Lord
Volume 2 – Here I Am to Worship
Volume 3 – How Great Is Our God
Volume 4 – He Is Exalted
Volume 5 – Joy to the World (Christmas)

Each volume features eight worship favorites that follow a similar theme for easy set selection. Bands can use the printed music and chord charts to play live together, and members can rehearse at home with the CD tracks. Worship leaders without a band can play/sing along with the CD for a fuller sound.

GUITAR WORSHIP METHOD SERIES

00695681 Guitar Worship Method 1
00699641 Guitar Worship Songbook 1
00695927 Guitar Worship Method 2
00701082 Guitar Worship Songbook 2
00696462 Guitar Worship – Chords

REFERENCE BOOKS

00331034 All About Music Technology in Worship

00330542 Church Sound Systems

00331468 The Ultimate Church Sound Operator's Handbook

Order from any music retailer, or visit www.halleonard.com.

7777 W. BLUEMOUND RD. P.O. BOX 13819 MILWAUKEE, WI 53213

Visit Hal Leonard Online at:
www.halleonard.com